Popular Mechanics

THE BOY MECHANIC SAVES THE WORLD

(ONE PROJECT *at a* TIME)

252 EARTH-FRIENDLY PROJECTS *and* TIPS

HEARST BOOKS

A division of Sterling Publishing Co., Inc.

New York / London

www.sterlingpublishing.com

Library of Congress Cataloging-in-Publication Data
The boy mechanic saves the world (one project at a time) : 252 Earth-friendly projects and tips.
     p. cm.
 "Popular Mechanics."
 Includes bibliographical references and index.
 ISBN 978-1-58816-772-9 (alk. paper)
 1. Handicraft for boys. 2. Energy conservation. 3. Recycling (Waste, etc.)
 4. Home economics. I. Popular mechanics (Chicago, Ill. : 1959)
 TT160.B795 2010
 745.5--dc22
                                    2009023229

10 9 8 7 6 5 4 3 2 1

Book design by Barbara Balch

Published by Hearst Books
A division of Sterling Publishing Co., Inc.
387 Park Avenue South, New York, NY 10016

Popular Mechanics is a registered trademark of Hearst Communications, Inc.

www.popularmechanics.com

For information about custom editions, special sales, premium and corporate purchases, please contact Sterling Special Sales Department at 800-805-5489 or specialsales@sterlingpublishing.com.

Distributed in Canada by Sterling Publishing
c/o Canadian Manda Group, 165 Dufferin Street
Toronto, Ontario, Canada M6K 3H6

Distributed in Australia by Capricorn Link (Australia) Pty. Ltd.
P.O. Box 704, Windsor, NSW 2756 Australia

Manufactured in China

Sterling ISBN 978-1-58816-772-9

CONTENTS

FOREWORD

Not so long ago, conservation was simply a way of life. Before today's superstores and online shopping made every imaginable home product so readily available, time- and energy-saving home solutions were handcrafted more often than bought. Nobody threw something out if it still had some life left in it. We were careful stewards of the great outdoors, because that's where we found our entertainment, relaxation, and escape.

So when we went searching through the Popular Mechanics archives for the best ideas from those simpler times, we found a wealth of environmentally friendly (and thrifty) projects: innovative creations from the turn of the last century, the war years, and the first stirrings of the environmental movement.

Looking back, we were reminded that when we had little, we learned how to repair or repurpose everyday items such as car tires and canning jars.

Here you'll find projects that demonstrate practical ways to protect the environment while getting things done—like how to trap garden and house pests humanely, and how to grow healthy gardens without using potent chemicals. Other topics show that basic home repairs can defer the expense of a new purchase—how to fix a loose table leg, or reweave the cane in old chairs; ways to use less fuel; and even new ways to use items that would otherwise be headed for the landfill, like turning ketchup bottles into soap dispensers, or tin cans into impromptu campsite ovens for baked potatoes.

Jump in and select topics that relate closest to your life. You may not have a garden, but we're pretty sure you've still had an occasional problem with mice. You may even find yourself constructing a backyard power-generating windmill. Every project undertaken is one step closer toward saving the world. (Or at least improving the health of the planet.)

The Editors of
Popular Mechanics

CHAPTER 1

IT'S YOUR ENVIRONMENT

USEFUL SHORTCUTS (*or* CONSERVING RESOURCES)

— STOP THE WASTE AND SAVE THE HEAT —

Keeping your home warm with less fuel and less of a heating bill need not be a big problem, because a lot of energy can be saved by doing many little things to keep the heat in and the cold out. But if the aggregate of little heat savers does not cut down your energy consumption sufficiently, you may have to resort to double-insulated windows, extra insulation, and automatic control instruments. Although these major energy savers are somewhat

HEAT IS LOST THROUGH AN OPEN FIREPLACE DAMPER.

costly, they may be necessary in some cases to maintain comfort with less energy than was consumed before.

Losses through negligence: Whether or not you provide insulated windows, sash windows, insulation, and control instruments, you can save considerable energy by avoiding carelessness in such simple things as leaving outside doors open longer than necessary, forgetting to close a furnace draft after adding fuel, forgetting to keep a fireplace draft shut when not in use, and neglecting to turn off radiators or registers in "open-air" bedrooms at night. Cold-air returns in an open bedroom should be shut off to prevent extremely cold air from entering. It is best to turn off the heat in a bedroom a few hours before retiring so that the temperature will decrease

TURN OFF THE BEDROOM RADIATOR AT NIGHT.

gradually, instead of attempting to chill the room suddenly and wasting heat through an open window. Space under a bedroom door should be blocked with a throw rug, folded blanket, or one of the many door draft blockers on the market to prevent cold air from circulating into the rest of the house.

More heat from radiators: Some heat can be saved by providing shields behind radiators that are set against uninsulated outside walls. Such shields, which prevent absorption of heat by the walls and consequent waste, may be of insulating or reflective material, or

A RUG SEALS THE CRACK UNDER A BEDROOM DOOR.

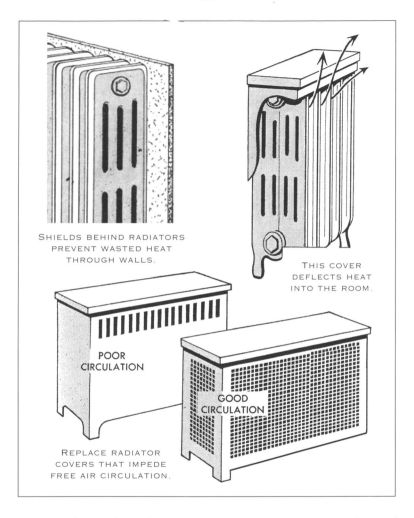

SHIELDS BEHIND RADIATORS
PREVENT WASTED HEAT
THROUGH WALLS.

THIS COVER
DEFLECTS HEAT
INTO THE ROOM.

POOR
CIRCULATION

GOOD
CIRCULATION

REPLACE RADIATOR
COVERS THAT IMPEDE
FREE AIR CIRCULATION.

simply hard-pressed board mounted so that there will be an air space of at least 1 in. between it and the wall. If your radiators are covered with boxes or grills that allow little circulation of air, you'll get more heat from the system by removing these impediments. Only those that do not impede the

USE ORDINARY OIL PAINT INSTEAD OF BRONZING FOR RADIATORS.

CAULK THE CRACKS BETWEEN DOOR AND WINDOW FRAMES.

ALSO CAULK BETWEEN WARPED SIDING.

free circulation of air are satisfactory. Also, keep dust and lint from accumulating in the open spaces by frequent cleaning to assure good air circulation. Paint on radiators has much more to do with the amount of heat that they radiate than most people suppose. If painted with bronzing, especially aluminum, they produce from 12 to 15 percent less heat than if painted with ordinary oil paint. Bronzing tends to reflect heat back into the radiator. Liberal use of caulking compound on all the cracks in the walls and around door and window frames will help to save some heat, whether or not the house is provided with storm sashes and is insulated. Cracks in brick and stucco walls should be filled with mortar.

— A Window Conservatory —

During the winter, when house-plants are kept inside, it is always a question how to arrange them so that they can get the necessary light without occupying too much room.

The sketch (*Figure 1*) shows how to make a neat window conservatory that can be built for a small cost. It can be fastened on the house just covering a window and will provide a fine place for the plants. The frame, shown in *Figure 2*, is made of about 2 x 2 in. material framed together as shown in *Figure 3*. This frame should be made

with the three openings of such a size that a four-paned sash, such as is used for a storm window, will fit nicely in them. If the four vertical pieces that are shown in *Figure 2* are dressed to the right angle, then it will be easy to put on the finishing corner boards that hold the sash.

The top and bottom are constructed with two small pieces, like the rafters, on which is nailed the sheathing boards. The shingles are then nailed on top and the finishing boards on the bottom.

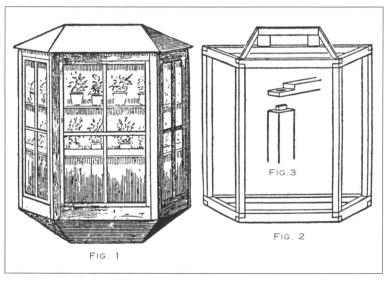

FIG. 1

FIG.3

FIG. 2

ARTISTIC WINDOW BOXES.

— Homemade Shower Bath —

While in the country during a long vacation, a traveler missed his daily bath, and so devised a shower bath that was completely satisfying. The back porch was enclosed with sheeting for the room, and the apparatus consisted of a galvanized-iron pail with a short nipple soldered in the center of the bottom and fitted with a valve and sprinkler. The whole, after filling the pail with water, was raised above the man's head with a rope run over a pulley fastened to the roof of the porch. A tub was used on the floor to catch the water. A knot should be tied in the rope at the right place, to keep it from running out of the pulley while

A WATER-CONSERVING SHOWER BATH
THAT CAN BE EASILY AND CHEAPLY MADE.

the pail is lowered to be filled with water. A loop should be made in the end, which is placed over a screw hook turned into the wall. If the loop is tied at the proper place, the pail will be raised to the right height for the person taking the shower bath.

The water will run from 10 to 15 minutes. The addition of some hot water will make for a splendid shower after a long day hiking. And, of course, such a shower uses far less water than any bath might, with just as much refreshment.

— A CLOTHESLINE REEL —

A clothesline can be a great way to save electricity and use the power of the sun, but the usual method of reeling up a clothesline and taking it in is quite a task. Many times the lines are left out in the open from one washday to another, due to neglect or forgetfulness. One innovative inventor created the arrangement shown in the sketch to take care of the line without any effort to the user.

All that is necessary to use this arrangement is to take the end of the line and run it over the hooks or sheaves on the posts, then secure it around an awning fastener. When let loose, the weight in the basement will wind up the line.

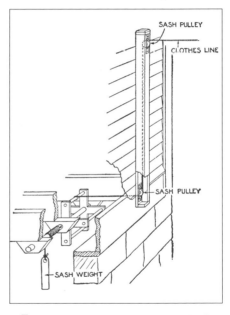

THE REEL DEVICE IN THE BASEMENT.

A knot can be tied in the line near the reel to catch at a hole in the sill, which will prevent strain on the reel. If the reel is made to wind up 4 ft. of line to each revolution and the sash-cord shaft is ⅜ in. in diameter, about 100 ft. of line can be taken up in a basement 7 ft. high.

— A Clothesline for Small Goods —

Handkerchiefs and small pieces included in the week's laundry are usually quite troublesome to hang with larger pieces. To solve this dilemma, one frustrated homeowner constructed a special line for small goods. A line was cut to fit between two porch posts, and hooks made of galvanized wire were tied to each end, staples being driven into the posts to receive the hooks. Three or four wire grips were formed and attached to the line. It was only necessary to draw the corner of a handkerchief into the grip as it was wrung out, placing several handkerchiefs in each grip.

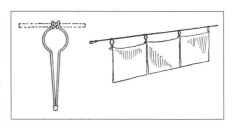

THE LINE AND HOLDERS ARE ALWAYS TOGETHER AND CAN BE WASHED WITH THE CLOTHES.

The line with its load was then carried out and attached between the porch posts. This made it unnecessary to look through the clothes for the small articles. It also prevented chilling the fingers, and no pins were needed.

— Miniature Hothouse Is Heated by Air from Basement —

Supported on a brick foundation in front of a basement window, this small hothouse uses heat from the basement to maintain an inside temperature suitable for growing plants. A thermostat inside the house controls a fan that blows in warm air when the outside temperature drops below freezing. In cold climates it may be necessary to bring air directly from the furnace to the hothouse.

Assemble the hothouse from window sashes, hinging the two sashes that form the roof to provide ventilation on warm days. All joints should be sealed against the entrance of cold air. Cleats may be fastened to the frames inside the end sash, if desired, to support narrow shelves for holding small flowerpots.

— A PERCOLATOR PUMP —

Don't bother wasting money and energy on a full-blown sump pump; shallow puddles on basement or bathroom floors are a cinch to sop up with this easy-to-make "percolator pump."

Drill a ¼-in. hole in the bottom of a 46-oz. juice can and through the center of a large, deep suction cup, such as that from a luggage rack. Cut a length of ¼-in.-OD brass tubing so that it passes almost through the cup and stands inside the can to about 1 in. from the top. Enlarge the hole in a ¾-in. neoprene faucet washer, and force it down on the tubing to hold the tube in place and seal the hole in the bottom of the can.

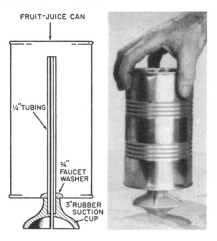

FRUIT-JUICE CAN

¼"TUBING

¾" FAUCET WASHER

3"RUBBER SUCTION CUP

Hand pressure operates the pump. The high tube eliminates the need for a check valve. After each stroke, lift the can to admit more water under the cup.

— DRYING SMALL LAUNDERED ARTICLES —

To save the energy mechanical drying uses, you should hang laundry out to dry. But the problem is the considerable time it takes to hang out a number of handkerchiefs, socks, napkins, etc. And very often the wind will blow many of them off the line. The task of drying these articles is made easy by using a bag of mosquito netting with the articles placed in it and hung on a line. The air can pass through the netting, and when the articles are dry, it does not take long to take them out.

AN EDGER, SIMILAR TO A GARDEN
PLOW, FOR QUICKLY TRIMMING THE SOD
AROUND A FLOWERBED.

— EDGING FLOWERBEDS
THE ECOLOGICALLY FRIENDLY WAY —

To improve the appearance of a flowerbed, it must be edged evenly and often. Because this became a tiresome task, one inspired gardener constructed an edger, as shown in the sketch. It consists of a wheel on a 4-ft. length of material measuring 2 x 4 in. in size. The material is made to taper and has a cross handle, 18 in. long, attached to its end. The wheel is 8 in. in diameter, and the cutter is attached, as shown, across the center of the wheel axle. This makes the edger turn easily on curves and corners. The cutter is 13 in. long

and turned under 1½ in. It is pushed along in the same manner as a garden cultivator.

― WATERING WINDOW-BOX FLOWERS ―

A window box for flowers can be conveniently watered in the following manner: Construct a metal box to receive the box holding the soil, and bore enough holes in its bottom to admit water to the soil. The inside box should be supported about 2 in. above the bottom of the metal box. Sponges are placed in the bottom to coincide with the holes in the soil box. A filling tube is made at the

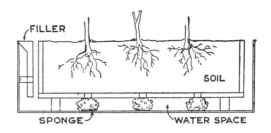

THE SOIL IS KEPT MOIST BY THE WATER FEEDING THROUGH THE SPONGES FROM THE UNDERSIDE.

end. The water is poured into the metal box, and the sponges admit only enough water for the plants, at all times.

― WATERING PLANTS AT THE ROOTS ―

An effective way to water rose bushes, shrubs, or other plants that might suffer if their leaves or stems are dampened for any length of time is to place an old cow horn in the earth so that the small end will be near the roots of the plant and the large end level with the surface of the ground. Just push it in and fill the horn with water. The small end of the horn should be cut off at such a point that the hole is about the size of a lead pencil. This will also help conserve against overwatering.

― RUSTIC TRELLIS TO SHADE DOOR OR WINDOW ―

Shade is a crucial part of keeping a home cool during the hotter months and helping reduce the cost of running the air conditioner. Proper preparation in the early spring will make it possible for the householder to shade doors and windows from the hot summer's sun, by means of inexpensive rustic trellises that add not a little to the beauty of the home. A suggestion for a trellis at a doorway and one for a window are shown in the illustration. They are made of straight tree trunks and small limbs, with the bark still on the wood. The curved portions of the window trellis may be made easily by using twigs that are somewhat green. Morning glories or other suitable climbing plants may be trained over the trellises.

WHEN COVERED WITH VINES, TRELLISES ADD TO THE CHARM OF THE HOME.

— Economy in Motorcycle Tires —

Caution in the use of motorcycle tires to ensure a minimum of abuse will result in considerable tire saving. Tremendous wear on a single spot results when the power is thrown in so suddenly that the driving wheel makes several revolutions before gripping the ground. The proper air pressure must be maintained in the tires in order to obtain good wear. Guessing is a poor method of determining the air pressure, and the exact condition should be noted from time to time with a gauge. Ordinarily, a pressure of 45 to 50 lb. should be maintained in the rear tire, and about 20 percent less in the front tire, in the case of 3-in. tires. Rim-cutting from running motorcycle tires under-inflated is the most common damage. Dents in the edge of the rims cause undue wear on the tire, the fabric being worn through by the constant rubbing. Bent rims are often caused by insufficient air pressure in tires, the liability to injury being increased when crossing tracks or bumps with an improperly inflated tire.

— Nine Ways to Stretch Your Fuel Dollar —

Unless your car is mechanically perfect and you're really an expert driver, there's little doubt that you can increase your miles-per-gallon average, depending on adjustments you make to your car and readjustments you are willing to make in your own driving habits. Here are nine gas-saving steps you can take:

1. Check all gas-line connections. Tighten up any that are loose, especially around the gas pump or injectors (or carburetor, if you have one). Any leakage of gasoline or loss by evaporation is wasteful.

2. Avoid needless idling. Three minutes of the engine idling and the car standing still uses as much as almost a half mile of driving at 30 mph.

3. Use a steady foot on the accelerator. When starting from a standing stop, press the gas pedal slowly and steadily; avoid jackrabbit starts and stops. "Flooring it" and then backing off burns up gas that isn't needed for acceleration. Maintain steady acceleration and deceleration at cruising speeds too (or, better yet, use cruise control whenever possible).

4. Use correct passing procedure. Never run up on the tail of the car ahead, slam on the brakes, and then hit the accelerator pedal hard to pass. Start your pass well back of the car ahead to permit a smooth swing—out and in again.

5. Drive at moderate speeds. Once the car shifts into driving gear, gas consumption increases as speed increases. Stay within posted speed limits; these are considered moderate as well as safe.

6. Don't brake unnecessarily. Try to time traffic lights, for example, so that you can keep rolling without stopping. You'll use more gas by stopping and starting again than if you can coast to the light just as it turns green and then re-apply a steady pressure on the gas pedal while you're still moving. When you must stop, let your engine act as a brake. Let up on the gas pedal at a sufficient distance from a stop sign to allow the engine to slow the car so that only a minimum use of brakes is needed. This conserves both gas and brakes.

7. With a manual transmission, use the brakes instead of the clutch when waiting for a light on an uphill grade. "Riding" the clutch and revving the engine to keep it from stalling wastes gas and increases wear on the clutch. Keep the clutch disengaged, or shift into neutral and use the brake.

8. Never fill the gas tank to the top, especially in hot weather. Gas expands as it heats up and may overflow a full tank. Always leave airspace of a few inches between the top of the gas and the top of the filler neck.

9. Slightly overinflate your tires. With less tire surface in contact with the road, less friction exists; thus, less gas is consumed. This doesn't mean you should jam 40 lb. of air into your tires; about 5 lb. over the recommended pressure is acceptable. Underinflation will substantially reduce tire life as well as rob your gas tank.

— EMERGENCY CAMP CONSTRUCTED ENTIRELY WITH AN AX —

An ax is the only tool needed to build a complete emergency camp for spending an unexpected night in the woods. With its help and a means of lighting a fire, you can be comfortable without blankets, even though the night is chilly. The first step in setting up the camp is to make a lean-to. For the uprights, use two 6-ft. saplings with forks, and set them firmly in the ground, spacing them about 7 ft. apart. Then cut a long pole and lay it across the forks. Four 6- or 7-ft. saplings are leaned with their ends resting on the cross pole. Then two or three poles are cut and laid across the leaning poles. The front of the lean-to is braced with two

10-ft. poles with forked ends, and all the poles are tied securely with strips of thin bark cut from a young tree.

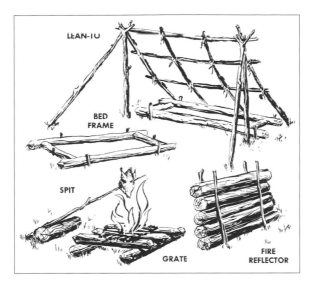

LEAN-TO

BED FRAME

SPIT

GRATE

FIRE REFLECTOR

Next, the bed frame is made from logs held in place by stakes driven in the ground. After this, gather pine or cedar branches. Lay the smaller branches in the bed frame to provide a soft mattress. Lay the larger branches in rows on the lean-to roof, with their tips downward, starting at the bottom and working up. Several layers of cedar branches will make the lean-to roof almost watertight.

A properly made campfire is extremely important. Because it must have plenty of draft, cut five small green logs about 4 ft. in length. Place two of these on the ground several feet in front of the lean-to, and lay the other three logs across the first two. Then build a fire of small, dry sticks on top of the logs so that the coals will fall between them and smolder, making a bed of coals for an all-night fire. If the night is cold or stormy, set up a reflector in back of the fire so that it will throw the heat into the lean-to. This is done by placing four or five green logs one on top of the other, holding them with four stakes driven into the ground. If you are fortunate enough to have some kind of meat, impale it on a spit and broil it over the fire. Use a limber green stick for the spit, and prop it over a small log to hold the meat far enough above the fire to permit cooking it without burning.

— UMBRELLA USED AS A CLOTHES DRYER —

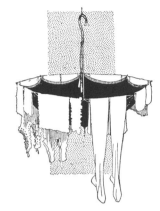

A clothes dryer that can be carried in a purse or a vest pocket will appeal to travelers and persons living in small quarters. An umbrella, four yards of strong wrapping twine, and several small brass rings are required. Knot the rings into the twine at intervals, measuring the distance between the rib points of the umbrella. Hook the twine to the points by the rings, as shown, providing considerable drying space for small articles. Hook the umbrella handle over a suitable support, or tie it carefully to the supporting pipe of a light fixture in the middle of the room, ready for the articles to be dried. The twine may also be wrapped around the points, but it is better to carry a line with rings attached.

— HOW TO FIGURE THE OPERATING COST OF ELECTRICAL APPLIANCES —

Have you ever wondered what it costs to operate certain electrical appliances, especially those that don't have the current rating stamped on the nameplate? To find out easily, turn off all appliances and turn on a few lamps of known wattage. Then count the number of revolutions that the disk in your electric meter makes in two minutes. Now turn off the lights and turn on the appliance

IT'S EASY TO FIGURE THE CURRENT CONSUMPTION OF ELECTRICAL APPLIANCES THAT DON'T HAVE THEIR WATTAGE ON THE NAMEPLATE.

for the same length of time, and count the revolutions of the meter disk. For example, say the wattage of the lamps was 700, and the disk made 70 revolutions in 2 minutes, and for the appliance it made 15 revolutions. Multiply 700 by 15, then divide by 70, which gives you 150, the watt-age of the appliance. Next, multiply this by the number of hours that the appliance operates per month, which gives watts consumed. Dividing this by 1,000 gives the kilowatts. Multiply this figure by the rate charged per kilowatt by your electric company.

— TEN TIPS FOR GETTING MORE OUT OF YOUR AIR-CONDITIONING —

An air conditioner is one of the big energy hogs in the home. A few useful strategies can lead to big savings on your energy and a better environment for everyone.

Outdoor temperature: Make sure your equipment is large enough to do the job. An air conditioner should have sufficient capacity to maintain a temperature of 75°F and 50 percent relative humidity within the space during the hottest days of the summer. Give or take a few degrees or percentage points, that's the level at which most people are comfortable.

This means that you would need a larger unit in Phoenix than you would for the same space in Chicago, because the hotter climate would require an additional 10 degrees or so of cooling capacity. Many people make the mistake of buying a unit that will cool the air by about 20 degrees, forget-ting that indoor cooling is directly related to the temperature outdoors. For real comfort, the climate has to be considered.

That "clammy" feeling: Make sure that your equipment isn't too large for the job. An oversize unit is often responsible for the feeling of "clamminess" found in some air-conditioned homes. The problem, of course, is excess humidity. A unit having too large a capacity will lower the temperature of the air quickly. Because the thermostat reads only temperature, it then turns the unit off. While the unit is off, the humidity climbs, along with the temperature. Another quick cooling cycle will drop the temperature but fail to remove enough of the accumulated moisture from the air. With each cycle, this condition becomes worse, until the air inside becomes muggy. You may actually be perspiring, though the air temperature is reasonably low.

A unit of the proper capacity will remain on long enough to lower the humidity to the desired level. During a heat wave, it may have to run almost constantly to control both temperature and humidity. But don't worry about the operating cost, because this relates more to the total heat removed than to the compressor operating time.

Storm windows: If you have them, leave your storm windows on throughout the summer. They can reduce the amount of heat entry through window glass in the same way they reduce heat loss in winter. This will mean less heat load for the air conditioner and results in lower operating costs. Sometimes, in fact, this little trick may make it possible to use a smaller air conditioner. One man saved nearly 15 percent on the cost of a central system by having his contractor refigure the cooling requirements based on the use of storm windows in summer.

Hands off that thermostat: Don't be a thermostat fiddler. This is especially important if you have central air-conditioning. When you leave the house, don't turn the air-conditioning off, figuring you'll turn it back on when you return. When you do this,

the unit must work overtime to cool down the house once you turn it back on again. Leave it at the same setting and you'll not only save money but also have a cool, comfortable house waiting for you.

It's even worse to turn off the air conditioner and fling open the windows when the first mild spell hits. Remember that when you turn on your air conditioner for the first time in early summer, the unit cools down the entire house, and everything in it—furniture, appliances, and rugs, plus 15 to 20 tons of building materials. If you turn the system off at the first sign of a cool spell, the temperature of the whole house will gradually rise again. Then, when the next heat wave hits, the air conditioner has to work overtime to cool everything down again. This results in increased operating costs.

You'll find that it's more efficient—and usually cheaper—to let the thermostat take over the whole job. During a cool spell, it will turn the compressor on just often enough to keep the house temperature under control. When hot weather returns, it will be better able to keep you comfortable.

Stored cooling: During a heat wave, lower your thermostat setting two or three degrees before going to bed. This is the only exception to the nofiddling-with-your-thermostat rule. The purpose is to store extra cooling potential in the furnishings and the building itself. This stored cooling will help fight off the high tide of heat that arrives the next day, especially during a really bad heat wave. Often, this can mean the difference between a cool house and the discomfort that results when your equipment doesn't have quite the capacity to fight off the soaring heat.

Use the same principle to prepare for a party. Extra people will put an extra load on your cooling system, so turn down the thermostat a few hours before your guests are scheduled to arrive. This head start will help your air conditioner cope with the increased load.

Insulation aids: Reduce heat buildup inside your house. Obviously, the more you can cut down on heat inside the house, the lighter the air-conditioning load. The roof is usually the biggest single source of heat entry, because of the sun boiling down on it all day. Thus, 6 in. of insulation in the attic floor will probably pay for itself by the heat it keeps out of the living quarters below. Large air vents at each end of the attic (or in the soffit) will allow natural breezes to wash out much of the hot attic air. If this fails to cool it down, try installing an exhaust fan.

Shades: good; awnings: better: Keep window shades or blinds drawn over the windows directly exposed to the hot sun. This is one of the simplest ways of keeping out heat. However, outside shading devices such as awnings and trees are about 50 percent better than interior shades in keeping heat out of a house. Remember this when landscaping.

Kitchen vent: Use a kitchen exhaust fan. Turn it on at times when the stove is being used. This will prevent cooking heat from spreading throughout the house and loading down your air-conditioning system unnecessarily. The best location for a kitchen exhaust fan is in the ceiling directly over the range, and the next best is in the wall above the range. Any other location will usually cut down on the fan's efficiency in getting rid of cooking heat.

Spring warm-up: With central air-conditioning, turn on the electricity one or two days before you start up the equipment in the spring. Today, nearly all central units have electric coils to warm the compressor. Switching on the electricity early will give the unit a chance to warm up before you use it. This not only avoids excessive wear but assures you of top operating efficiency right from the start.

Room conditioners: Know how you can "stretch" a room air conditioner. You can't turn it into a central system, but you can take advantage of its full capacity. Be sure to adjust the air outlet vanes so that cool air isn't being short-circuited back to the intake. If you have a warm-air heating system, close off all hot-air registers and cool-air return ducts in the room where you're using the air conditioner. Otherwise you'll lose cool air through the heating system ducts. Because most room air conditioners have a relatively small capacity, such leaks may make it impossible for the unit to cool even one large room during a hot spell. Finally, it's often possible to cool a whole section of the house with one such unit, particularly if the weather isn't hot enough to require full capacity to cool one room. Use a ventilating fan to distribute the cool air from one room to another.

ENERGY SOLUTIONS

— HOW TO MAKE A WINDMILL OF 1 OR 2 HORSEPOWER FOR PRACTICAL PURPOSES —

A windmill for developing from ½ to 2 hp. may be constructed at home, the expense being very small and the results highly satisfactory.

The hub for the revolving fan wheel is constructed first. A good way to get the hub, lining, shaft, and spokes for the blades is to purchase the wheel and axle of some old cart rig from a wheelwright or junk dealer. There are always a number of discarded carriages, wagons, or parts thereof in the rear of the average blacksmith's shop. Remove all but the four

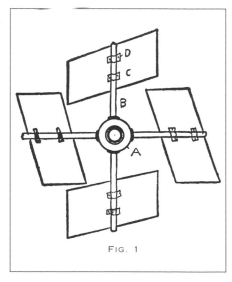

FIG. 1

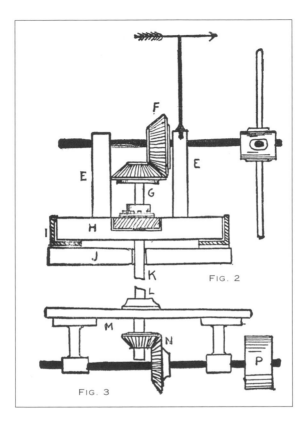

FIG. 2

FIG. 3

spokes needed for the fans from the wheel, as in *Figure 1*. The same hub, axle, and bearings will do. If you cannot secure a wheel and shaft, the hub may be made from a piece of hardwood about 4 in. in diameter and 6 in. long. A 2-in. hole should be bored through for a wooden shaft, or a 1½ in. hole for a metal shaft. The hub may be secured by putting two or three metal pins through the hub and shaft. Adjust the spokes by boring holes for them, and arrange them so that they extend from the center *A*, like *B*. The wheel is then ready for the blades. These blades should be of sheet metal or thin hardwood. The sizes may vary according to the capacity of the wheel and amount of room for the blades on the spokes. Each one is tilted so as to receive the force of the wind at an angle. This adjustment causes the wheel to revolve when the wind pressure is strong enough. Secure the blades to the spokes by using little metal cleats, *C* and *D*. Bend these metal strips to suit the form of the spokes, and flatten against the blades. Then insert the screws to fasten the cleats to the wood. If sheet-metal blades are used, rivets should be used for fastening them.

The stand for the wheel shaft is shown in *Figure 2*. Arrange the base piece in platform order, per *J*. This is more fully shown in *Figure 5*. Place the seat or ring for the revolving table on top of this base piece, which is about 36 in. long. The circular seat is indicated at *I*, *Figure 2*. This ring is like an inverted cheesebox cover with the center cut out. It can be made by a tinsmith. The outside ring diameter is 35 in., and the shoulders are 4 in. high and made of tin also. Form the shoulder by soldering the piece on. Thus we get a smooth surface with sides for the mill base to turn in, so as to receive the wind at each point to advantage. The X-shaped piece *H* rests in the tin rim. The X form, however, does not show in this sketch, but in *Figure 5*, where it is marked *S*. This part is made of two pieces of 2-in. plank, about 3 in. wide, arranged so that the two pieces cross to form an X. Where the pieces join, mortise them one into the other so as to secure a good joint. Adjust the uprights for sustaining the wheel shaft to the X pieces, as shown at *EE*, *Figure 2*. These are 4 x 4 in. pieces of wood, hard pine preferred, planed and securely set up in the X pieces by mortising into the same. Make the bearings for the wheel shaft in the uprights and insert the shaft.

The gearing for the transmission of the power from the wheel shaft to the main shaft below, calculated for the delivery of the power at an accessible point, must next be adjusted. The windmill is intended for installation on top of a building, and the power may be transmitted below, or to the top of a stand specially erected for the purpose. It is wise to visit a secondhand machinery dealer and get four gears, a pulley, and a shaft. Gears about 5 in. in diameter and beveled will be required. Adjust the first pair of the beveled gears as at *F* and *G*. If the wheel shaft is metal, the gear may be set-screwed to the shaft or keyed to it. If the shaft is hardwood, it will be necessary to arrange for a special connection. The

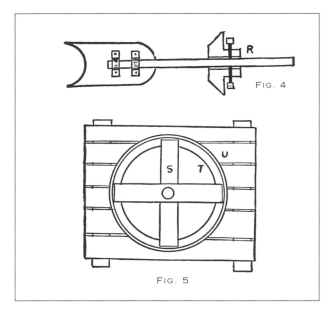

FIG. 4

FIG. 5

shaft may be wrapped with sheet metal, and this metal fastened on with screws. Then the gear may be attached by passing a pin through the setscrew hole and through the shaft. The upright shaft is best made of metal. This shaft is shown extending from the gear, *G*, to a point below. The object is to have the shaft reach to the point where the power is received for the service below. The shaft is shown cut off at *K*. Passing to *Figure 3*, the shaft is again taken up at *L*. It now passes through the arrangement shown, and the device is rigged up to hold the shaft and

delivery wheel *P* in place. This shaft should also be metal. Secure the beveled gears *M* and *N* as shown. These transmit the power from the upright shaft to the lower horizontal shaft. Provide the wheel or pulley *P* with the necessary belt to carry the power from this shaft to the point of use.

The tailboard of the windmill is illustrated in *Figure 4*. A good way to make this board is to use a section of thin lumber and attach it to the rear upright, as shown in *E*, *Figure 2*. This may be done by boring a hole in the upright and inserting the shaft of the tailpiece. In *Figure 4* is also

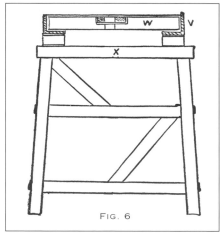

FIG. 6

whenever the wind alters and causes the wheel's position to change. The ring and ring base are secured to the platform, *U*. The latter is made of boards nailed to the timbers of the staging for supporting the mill. This staging is shown in *Figure 6*, in a sectional view. The ring with its X piece is marked *V*; the X piece is marked *W*; and the base for the part and the top of the stage is marked *X*. The stage is made of 2 x 4 in. stock. The height may vary, according to the requirements. If the affair is set up on a barn or shed, the staging will be sufficient to support the device. But if the stage is constructed direct from the ground, it will be necessary to use some long timbers to get the wheel up high enough to receive the benefit of the force of the wind. Proceeding on the plan of the derrick stand, as shown in *Figure 6*, a stage of considerable height can be obtained.

shown the process of fastening a gear, *R*, to the shaft. The setscrews enter the hub from the two sides, and the points are pressed upon the shaft, thus holding the gear firmly in place. The platform for the entire wheel device is shown in *Figure 5*. The X piece *S* is bored through in the middle, and the upright shaft passes through. The tin runway or ring is marked *T*, and the X piece very readily revolves in this ring

— HOW TO MAKE A MINIATURE WINDMILL —

The following describes the construction of a miniature windmill that provided considerable power for its size, even in a light breeze. Its smaller parts, such as blades and pulleys, were constructed of 1-in. sugar pine, on account of its softness.

The eight blades were made from 1 x 1½ x 12 in. pieces. Two opposite edges were cut away until the blade was about ⅛ in. thick. Two

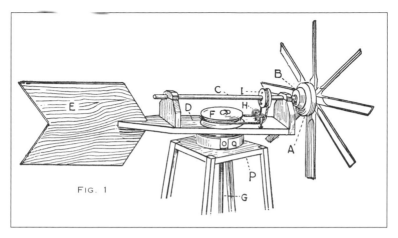

FIG. 1

THE FINISHED WINDMILL.

inches were left uncut at the hub end. They were then nailed to the circular faceplate, *A*, *Figure 1*, which is 6 in. in diameter and 1 in. thick. The center of the hub was lengthened by the wooden disk, *B*, *Figure 1*, which was nailed to the faceplate. The shaft, *C*, *Figure 1*, was ¼-in. iron rod, 2 ft. long, and turned in the bearings detailed in *Figure 2*. *J* was a nut from a wagon bolt and was placed in the bearing to ensure easy running. The bearing blocks are 3 in. wide, 1 in. thick, and 3 in. high without the upper half. Both bearings were made in this manner.

Shaft *C* was keyed to the hub of the wheel, as shown in *Figure 3*. A staple, *K*, holds the shaft from revolving in the hub. This method is also applied in keying the 5-in. pulley, *F*, to the shaft, *G*, *Figure 1*, which extends to the ground. The 2½ in. pulley, *I*, *Figure 1*, is keyed to shaft *C*, as shown in *Figure 4*. Wire *L* was put through the hole in the axle and the two ends curved so as to pass through the two holes in the pulley, after which they were given a final bend to keep the pulley in place. The method by which shaft *C* was kept from working forward is shown in *Figure 5*. The washer, *M*, intervenes between the bearing block and wire *N*, which is passed through the axle and then bent to prevent its falling out. Two washers are placed on shaft *C*, between the forward bearing and the hub of the wheel, to lessen the friction.

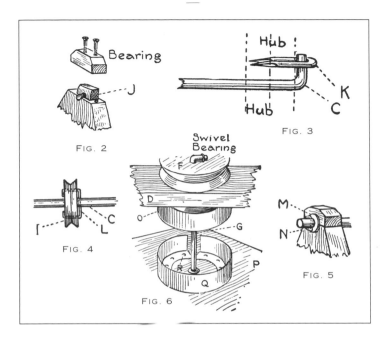

Bearing

FIG. 2

FIG. 3

Swivel Bearing

FIG. 4

FIG. 5

FIG. 6

The bedplate *D, Figure 1,* is 2 ft. long, 3 in. wide, and 1 in. thick, and is tapered from the rear bearing to the slot in which the fan, *E,* is nailed. This fan is made of ¼-in. pine sized 18 x 12 in. and is cut to the shape shown.

The two small iron pulleys with screw bases, *H, Figure 1,* were obtained for a small sum from a hardware dealer. The diameter of each is 1¼ in. The belt that transfers the power from shaft *C* to shaft *G* is top string, with a section of rubber in it to take up slack. To prevent

it from slipping on the two wooden pulleys, a rubber band is placed in the grooves of each.

The point for the swivel bearing was determined by balancing the bedplate, with all parts in place, across the thin edge of a board. At that point a ¼-in. hole was bored, in which shaft *G* turns. Washers are placed under pulley *F* to lessen the friction there. The swivel bearing is made from two lids of baking powder cans. A section is cut out of one to permit its being enlarged enough to admit the other. The smaller one,

O, *Figure 6,* is nailed, top down, with the sharp edge to the underside of the bedplate so that the ¼-in. hole for the shaft G is in the center. The other lid, G, is tacked, top down also, in the center of board P, with brass-headed furniture tacks, R, *Figure 6.* These act as a smooth surface on which the other tin revolves. Holes for shaft G are cut through both lids. Shaft G is but ¼ in. in diameter, yet to keep it from rubbing against board P, a ½-in. hole is bored for it through the latter.

The tower is made of four 1 x 1 in. strips, 25 ft. long. They converge, from points on the ground forming an 8-ft. square, to board P at the top of the tower. This board is 12 in. square, and the corners are notched to admit the strips, as shown in *Figure 1.* Laths are nailed diagonally between the strips to strengthen the tower laterally. Each strip is screwed to a stake in the ground; thus, by disconnecting two of them the other two can be used as hinges, and the tower can be tipped over and lowered to the ground. This is handy when, for instance, the windmill needed oiling. Bearings for shaft G are placed 5 ft. apart in the tower.

The windmill's power has been put to various uses.

— HOW TO MAKE A STATIONARY WINDMILL —

A windmill that can be made stationary and that will run regardless of the direction of the wind is illustrated in *Figure 1.* Mills of this kind can be built of a larger size, and in some localities have been used for pumping water.

Two semicircular surfaces are secured to the axle at right angles to each other and at 45-degree angles to that of the axle, as shown in *Figure 2.* This axle and wings are

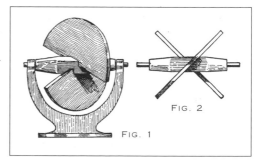

FIG. 2

FIG. 1

RUNS IN WIND FROM ANY DIRECTION.

mounted in bearings on a solid or stationary stand or frame. By mounting a pulley on the axle with the wings, it can be used to run toy machinery.

— A Novel and Effective Garden Mulcher —

Just because a garden plot is free of weeds, it does not necessarily follow that it is sufficiently cultivated; if the soil becomes hard, packed by the rain and baked by the sun, the garden's vegetables or flowers will not thrive. Consequently, it is absolutely necessary that the topsoil be kept loose if the plants are to develop in the manner that they should.

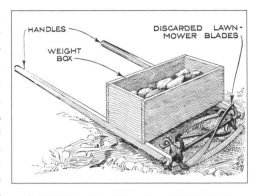

A GARDEN MULCHER AND WEEDER THAT CAN BE PUSHED ALONG BETWEEN ROWS OF GROWING PLANTS IS EASILY MADE FROM THE REVOLVING BLADES OF AN OLD LAWN MOWER.

For this purpose, a revolving mulcher, made from the cutter reel of a discarded lawn mower, will be found better and easier to operate than a hoe. To construct such a mulcher, make a pair of handles from strong material, and mount the cutter reel across the ends of the handles. Just back of the handles a box is made to hold as many stones or other weights as will be necessary to cause the mulcher to cut to the proper depth. In use, the tool is pushed or pulled between the rows. The blades will revolve and cut into the soil and, due to the arrangement of the cutters, the ground will be loosened and stirred up quite effectively.

— Spit Turned by Water Power —

Many of the peasants and rural residents around the world do their cooking in the open air over bonfires. You can do the same if you live near a river or tend to spend a good deal of time near one quite often. The illustration here shows a laborsaving machine in use that enables the cook to go away and leave meat roasting for an hour at a time.

The illustration also shows how the spit to which the meat is fastened is constantly turned by means of a slowly moving waterwheel. You may wish to try the scheme when camping out. Its success depends upon a slow current; a fast-turning wheel will burn the meat.

GROW YOUR OWN

— BRACING SAVES OLD TREES —

B efore you cut down the venerable shade tree that's showing signs of old age, take time to examine it closely. Cabling and rod bracing may save it for many more years of usefulness by providing mechanical support for weakened branches.

Tight V-crotches are a frequent source of trouble in both young and old trees that grow with multiple, or divided, trunks. Major limbs that begin growth very nearly parallel to each other often develop a seam or joint or nonconnecting tissue at the division point. This results from the squeezing and crushing of the cambium layer and bark as growth progresses. Eventually the affected tissues die, leaving an open seam.

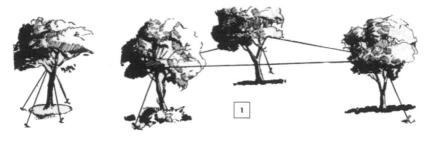

WHERE TREES OF THE SAME AGE ARE GROUPED CLOSELY TOGETHER, INTERTREE CABLING IS FREQUENTLY USED TO STABILIZE GROWTH AND AID TOP FORMATION. LARGE INDIVIDUAL TREES ARE OFTEN GUYED WITH CABLES, AS IN THE LEFT-HAND DETAIL.

When the limbs become loaded with ice, or when the foliage is thoroughly wet down by a heavy rainstorm, the joint may break and cause irreparable damage to the tree.

A second-ranking source of trouble in older trees is a decayed or damaged trunk caused by a fungus attack or only partially healed wounds. Sometimes trunks and large limbs will be split by the twisting stresses of high winds or sleet storms. Such damage should be repaired immediately, or the tree will be lost.

The two general methods of tree bracing are cabling and rod bracing. Although each tree will present its own particular challenges, the two methods have several common applications. Where younger trees stand in close proximity, intertree cabling combined with rodding, *Figure 1,* is frequently used to stabilize them and promote proper top formation. In older trees the methods are sometimes combined to distribute stresses that might cause damage to the individual trees, especially in open, windswept locations, such as on large lawns or estates.

Utilizing the same principle, interbranch cabling of several types is used to support the tops of large individual trees. Typical applications are shown in *Figure 2.* The cables are installed high in the branches, to equalize the load on structurally weak crotches. As a rule, the most efficient system for general use is the triangular system, *Figure 2.* When the cables are installed, care must be taken to locate them so that they do not touch other branches or the trunk of the tree, because damage may result.

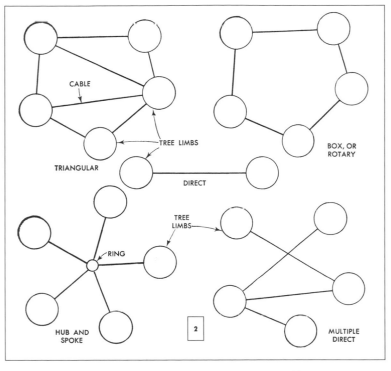

CABLE

TREE LIMBS

TRIANGULAR

BOX, OR ROTARY

DIRECT

TREE LIMBS

RING

HUB AND SPOKE

2

MULTIPLE DIRECT

DETAILS SHOWING COMMON METHODS OF CABLING. THIS TYPE OF CABLING ALSO PREVENTS DAMAGE DURING HIGH WINDS.

The location of the cables in relation to the length of the branches depends to some extent on the structure of the tree, but it's a safe rule to place the screw eyes, or lags, about two-thirds the distance from the crotch to the end of the limb. Holes for the screw eyes should be drilled so that when the eyes are installed, the parts will be in a straight line.

Otherwise the screw eyes will be bent when subjected to strain. After measuring the distance between the screw eyes to determine the length of each cable, the cable should be cut to length and eye-spliced, as in *Figure 4, A, B, C,* and *D.* For average spans, ¼-in. cable is suitable for supporting limbs up to 6 in. in diameter. For larger limbs, use 5/16- or 3/8-in. cable.

PARALLEL RODS

SINGLE BOLT

3

DETAILS OF RODDING LARGE LIMBS
WITHIN THE TREETOP TO SUPPORT
A SPREADING TOP AND PREVENT
CROTCH BREAKAGE.

After installation, the cables should be under sufficient tension to hold taut when the limbs are swayed by wind. To accomplish this, the limbs

are roped to the tree trunk and raised somewhat above their normal position before cabling. In some cases this will require the aid of a tackle block.

Figure 3 illustrates three methods of rod bracing in common use. To avoid weakening the limbs, the single-bolt method is the most widely used, as it requires drilling only one hole in each of the affected limbs. The rod used is continuously threaded with a square thread similar to a lag screw. Usually it is cadmium-plated and comes in sizes ranging from ⅝ to 1 in. in diameter. Ordinarily, a hole slightly smaller than the diameter of the rod is drilled through both limbs to a point ranging from 18 to 36 in. above the crotch, and the rod is turned in until one end projects an inch or so. Then it is cut off to the required length and the ends coated with a special tree-wound tar.

In some cases, when the limbs are exceptionally large, it will be necessary to countersink diamond-shaped washers, or plates, over both ends of the rod and to draw tight with nuts, as in the detail in *Figure 5*. In making the countersinks, use a sharp chisel to produce a clean wound that will heal quickly. Fill the countersinks with tree-wound tar.

Split trunks and large limbs are sometimes salvaged through the use

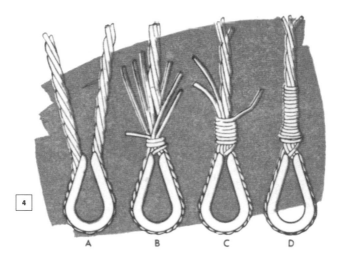

CABLES ANCHORED TO LIMBS WILL REQUIRE AN EYE SPLICE AT EACH
END. DETAILS SHOW HOW TO MAKE A SEVEN-WIRE SPLICE.

of lip and cross bolts installed across the break, as in the upper details in *Figure 5*. Large, hollow trunks are frequently braced in this manner before being filled with tree cement. In order to be fully effective, rods used without nuts and washers should be turned into at least 4 in. of sound wood in small trees and 6 in. of wood in larger trees. It's a good idea to coat the rods with tree tar before turning them into place.

In some rare instances it is desirable to bolt two limbs tightly together, or a few inches apart, as in the details in *Figure 5*. Usually this is done to preserve for a time the form of an old tree. In younger trees one of the interfering limbs should be removed. The limbs should never be forced together and bolted. Only when they are touching at some point is it permissible to insert the bolt without a spacer. In some cases they are separated and bolted together with a spacer between, as in the center detail.

Large limbs that rub together during windstorms can be separated by means of the slide arrangement shown in the lower detail in *Figure 5*. A strip or block of hardwood is bolted to one of the limbs, preferably the lower

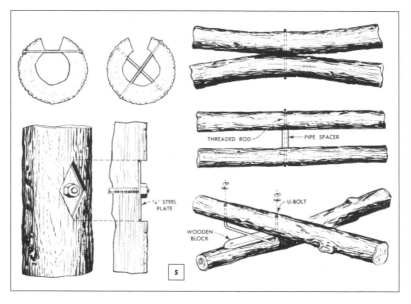

IN MANY INSTANCES, SPLIT LIMBS AND HOLLOW TRUNKS OF
OLDER TREES ARE REINFORCED BY LIP AND CROSS-BOLTING.
SPECIAL THREADED RODS ARE USED FOR THIS TYPE
OF BRACING ON BOTH OLD AND YOUNG TREES.

one, and a long U-bolt made from smooth steel rod is fitted into two holes drilled in the upper limb, as shown. Thread both ends of the rod before bending, the thread length being slightly greater than the diameter of each limb. After the rod has been bent into the U shape, run nuts down to the limit of the threads on both ends, and place washers over the nuts. Then insert the bolt in the holes and turn nuts onto the projecting ends, as shown. It is of the utmost importance to treat all tree wounds immediately, to prevent the entrance of insects and disease-producing organisms. Wounds made by cutting through the bark into the cambium layer must be sealed at once with a special dressing made for the purpose, or with a dressing made by mixing dry Bordeaux with raw linseed oil; the paste should be sufficiently heavy to stay in place when spread with a putty knife or small trowel. Discard the unused portion of this mixture.

— OPERATION "HEAD START" —

Spring is the time not only to plan a garden but also to get a head start with seedlings so that your "crops" are ready weeks ahead of time. If you missed out this year, here is how to move your garden schedule ahead in future years.

For growing young plants from seed, a cold frame, as shown in *Figure 1*, is the answer if you have enough room. A stock window sash, available at most lumberyards, is hinged to a box built of pressure-treated lumber. An underground cable brings in house current to a weather-tight receptacle that furnishes electricity to a "lift-out" board holding four 60-W lamps, to provide heat on chilly nights

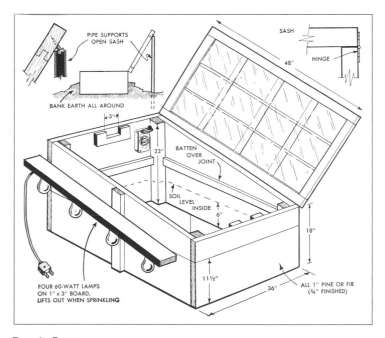

FIG. 1: PRODUCE FROM YOUR GARDEN CAN BE ON YOUR TABLE WEEKS AHEAD OF TIME IF YOU BUILD THE COLD FRAME SHOWN HERE. SEEDS PLANTED EARLY WILL BE YOUNG PLANTS BY THE TIME THE WEATHER IS WARM ENOUGH TO PERMIT THEIR PLANTING OUTSIDE.

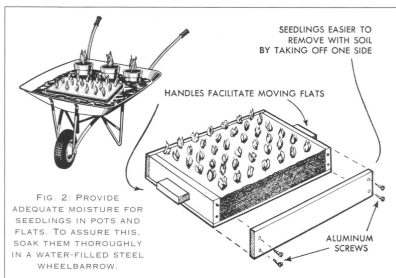

SEEDLINGS EASIER TO
REMOVE WITH SOIL
BY TAKING OFF ONE SIDE

HANDLES FACILITATE MOVING FLATS

FIG. 2: PROVIDE
ADEQUATE MOISTURE FOR
SEEDLINGS IN POTS AND
FLATS. TO ASSURE THIS,
SOAK THEM THOROUGHLY
IN A WATER-FILLED STEEL
WHEELBARROW.

ALUMINUM
SCREWS

FIG. 3: IF YOU BUILD YOUR OWN FLATS,
ASSEMBLE AS SHOWN. THE HANDLES
MAKE FOR EASIER LIFTING AND
THE REMOVABLE SIDES ALLOW
FOR TRANSPORTING.

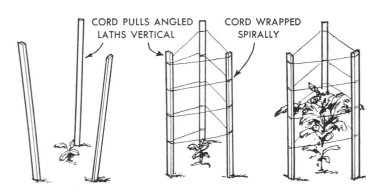

CORD PULLS ANGLED
LATHS VERTICAL

CORD WRAPPED
SPIRALLY

FIG. 4: SUPPORTS FOR TOMATO PLANTS REQUIRE
ONLY A FEW LATHS AND SOME HEAVY CORD.

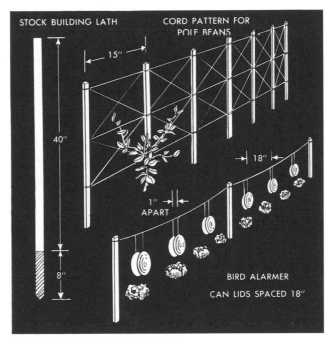

STOCK BUILDING LATH

CORD PATTERN FOR
POLE BEANS

15"

40"

18"

1"
APART

BIRD ALARMER

CAN LIDS SPACED 18"

8"

FIG. 5: LATH AND HEAVY CORD ARE ALSO USED FOR A
"FENCE" ON WHICH POLE BEANS CAN GROW. LIDS
SAVED FROM FOOD TINS ARE STRUNG IN PAIRS
TO FRIGHTEN AWAY HUNGRY BIRDS.

and sunless days. The weather-tight receptacle is closed when plants in the frame are sprinkled.

If you have no room for a cold frame, wooden flats, *Figure 3,* and clay pots can be located in a basement or utility room for the starting of seedlings. It is best to give the seedlings a good soaking once a week, rather than a daily sprinkling. This is true especially in homes with forced-air heat, where low humidity will cause fast evaporation.

A metal wheelbarrow filled with water will permit giving flats and pots a thorough soaking, as shown in *Figure 2.* Whether you make your own flats or buy them, fix one side of each unit so that it can be removed, as indicated in *Figure 3.* Each seedling, with its necessary ball of soil, can then be removed readily.

Provide support for tomato plants full of heavy, ripe fruit by driving three lengths of wood lath around each plant as it is set out. String heavy cord, *Figure 4,* to support the mature plants. Pole beans require a fence of cord and laths, as shown in *Figure 5.*

For all plants, tin-can lids strung as indicated in the lower detail in *Figure 5* will help keep away hungry birds. Every whisper of wind will blow the lids together noisily and spin them so that the sun will glitter on their shiny surfaces.

— FIVE WAYS TO MAKE YOUR OWN FERTILIZER —

If the high cost of garden fertilizers has discouraged you from developing a "green thumb," here are several ways of producing all of the natural fertilizer you'll need at no cost. Simply build one of the five types of compost enclosures illustrated, and keep it filled with lawn clippings and other vegetable-waste matter.

The type of enclosure you build and the materials you use for its construction are unimportant. However, compost matter should be piled as high as possible to minimize evaporation and to retain heat generated by the microorganisms that reduce the material to fertilizer. For these reasons, do not build a composter that is too large for your needs.

An efficient composter is one that rapidly converts vegetable matter into

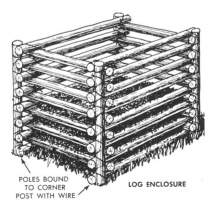

POLES BOUND TO CORNER POST WITH WIRE   **LOG ENCLOSURE**

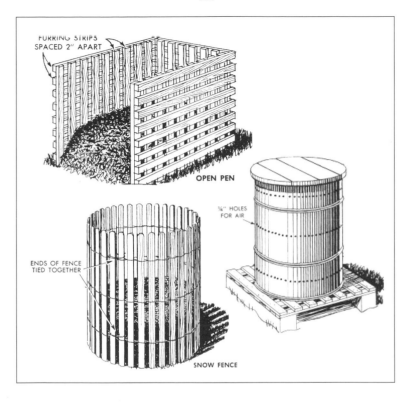

FURRING STRIPS SPACED 2" APART

OPEN PEN

ENDS OF FENCE TIED TOGETHER

¾" HOLES FOR AIR

SNOW FENCE

dark-colored, granular fertilizer that has an odor of good, rich earth. Five elements are necessary to accomplish this: vegetable matter, moisture, air, warmth, and microorganisms.

Bulky plants such as tomato vines and weeds should be chopped into small pieces to permit the compost to be packed more densely, which induces faster decomposition. If the material is dry, saturate it with water.

To keep the compost sweet smelling there must be adequate exposure to the atmosphere. Each of the five types of enclosures shown provides for ample ventilation. Heat is developed by the microorganisms working on the compost materials, in the process developing temperatures as high as 165°F in a densely compacted, bacteria-rich mixture. In addition to the speeding of decomposition, the high temperatures will kill germs and weed seeds. The best procedure for filling a composter is to first throw a 2-in. layer of moist grass on the bottom. Then sprinkle a thin layer of black soil on top. The soil provides the microorganisms (bacteria and fungi) needed for decomposition.

Continue filling the composter, alternating a layer of vegetable waste with a layer of soil. For extra rich compost, sprinkle soil layers with bone meal, ground rock phosphate, or lime. In two to four weeks most of the vegetable matter should be converted to rich fertilizer.

— A WINDOW GREENHOUSE —

The drawing shows a simple window greenhouse that can be easily erected from ordinary window sashes, assembled and fastened to the sill, top, and sides of the window casing. The roof is also a sash, but is hinged at the back, next to the house, so that it can be raised in fine weather. A cord attached to an angular bar, which is pivoted to the side as indicated, is used for raising or lowering the top.

A window greenhouse should preferably be placed on the south side of the house, so as to get the full benefit of the sunlight. Shelves and brackets can be fitted inside for the accommodation of plants that have trailing or drooping habits. Sufficient heat will be furnished from the room to make the growing of hard plants an easy matter. Among these are violets, pansies, English daisies, lettuce, parsley, radishes, and in fact,

any flower or small vegetable that can be grown in the early spring and late fall in cold frames.

If desired, the greenhouse may be made so that it can be taken apart and the various parts stored away during the summer.

— GROWING LARGE GRAPES —

By making use of a method not widely known, fruits of large size can be obtained from trees and vines. The idea is based on certain characteristics of the sap flow in the plants. The sap that contains the plant nourishment goes up into the outer cells of the sapwood; it descends late in the season, not through the same cells but through the large so-called sieve cells of the inner bark.

A prize-winning bunch of grapes was produced by an application of this knowledge in the following manner: The grower first selected a perfect bunch of grapes growing from a good, strong cane. Next, he cut off all bunches above it on the same cane, and just below the selected cluster the cane was girdled, the bark being removed in a band about 1 in. wide. A paper bag was then pinned over the bunch.

When the sap started back along the canes to the roots, it was richly laden with the starch manufactured by the leaves. Ordinarily this nourishment would go largely to the roots, there to be stored. In this case, however, the ring of bark that was removed acted as a dam, beyond which the downward-flowing sap could not pass. Consequently the sap was backed up and converted into fruit, which would naturally be larger than normal.

The professional horticulturist calls this method "ringing," and there are other ways in which it can be applied to special situations. It is a fact observed by fruit growers that a very heavy crop that bends the branches of an apple tree far down seems to establish the bearing habit, so afterward the tree will bear unusually well. The scientific explanation is that the bending down of the branches has constricted the inner bark, and the downward flow of sap is distinctly below normal.

A selected branch of a fruit tree can be made to bear better by twisting a wire around it. A young apple tree can be brought into bearing earlier than normal in the same manner, and a backward pear tree can be stimulated to fruit by weighting down the ends of the long branches in summer and throughout the dormant winter period. This will often force productiveness the next year. The secret of the abnormally large pears, apples, and other fruits grown on dwarf trees lies in this general principle; an imperfect union at the grafting point prevents the normal downward flow of sap, and the dammed-up plant food goes into the fruit.

— GRAPE ARBOR BUILT OF POLES —

Rustic outdoor structures constructed from fallen trees are excellent alternatives to expensive store-bought varieties. In building structures such as arches, grape arbors, or pergolas, it is not even necessary to use sawed lumber, because they can easily be built just as substantially, and frequently more artistically and cheaply, using poles.

Poles are usually easy to obtain, especially in the country or in the smaller cities where there are usually many trees and gardens from which branches must be pruned or from which they fall naturally. Large parks are also good sources of fallen branches that can be used for poles.

The grape arbor illustrated here consists of but one row of uprights. Across the top of each is placed a horizontal support for the roof poles, as shown in, which is carried near its outer end by an inclined brace. The brace should be connected at each end with a toe joint, as shown in *Figure 2*. The upper end of the upright is beveled off on both sides to form a double-splayed joint with the crosspiece. To securely bind the roof of the arbor, the long poles, or roof beams, should be notched near each end to fit over the supports. Similar notches

FIG. 1

FIG. 2

in the poles forming the sides of the arbor are to fit the uprights, thereby binding them together and preventing toppling over. Each set of long poles connecting two uprights should have the end notch the same distance apart, one pole being used as a gauge. All the joints and notches may be cut with a sharp hatchet.

In setting the arbor, the uprights should first be assembled, complete with braces and roof supports, and placed in the ground at a distance apart corresponding to that of the notches on the long poles. The uprights being set, the long poles are placed and fastened with nails.

— How to Build a Simple Grape Arbor of Wood —

One of the most attractive features you can install in a garden is a simple grape arbor. Used for grapes, it brings to mind a lovely vineyard, but it can also be used for climbers of any kind, from pole beans to morning glories.

A grape arbor made of white pine, put together as shown in the sketch, will last for several years. The 2 x 4 in. posts, *A*, are 7 ft. long. The feet, *B*, are made 2 x 4 in., 4 ft. long, and rest on a brick, *C*, placed under each end. The construction, although simple and easy to follow, will be sturdy and durable. As the vines

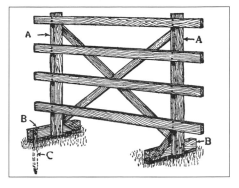

GRAPE-ARBOR TRELLIS.

wrap around the small arbor, they will further secure and stabilize its structure. Over time, the appearance will become weathered and even more attractive than when first constructed.

— Irrigating with Tomato Cans —

The following is an easy and effective way to start plants in dry weather: Sink an ordinary tomato can, with an ⅛-in. hole ½ in. from the bottom, into the ground so that the hole will be near the roots of the plant. Tamp the dirt around both plant and can, and fill the latter with water. Keep the can filled until the plant is out of danger.

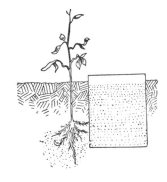

— UMBRELLA USED AS A FLOWER TRELLIS —

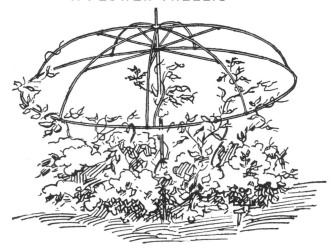

FRAME SUPPORTING A VINE

The garden is often one of the best places to reuse ruined or soon-to-be-discarded household items. Simply procure a collapsed, discarded umbrella and then remove the cloth, leaving only the steel frame. Join the ends of the ribs by running a fine wire through the tip of each rib and giving it one turn around to hold them at equal distances apart. You will then insert the handle into the ground and some climbing vine will be planted beneath it. The plant will climb all over the steel frame and make a very attractive garden piece sure to be noticed.

— DRYING AND SAVING SEEDS —

A good way to dry tomato, cantaloupe, and other seeds is to put them on blotters. They will quickly dry in this manner and will not become moldy, because the blotter soaks up the moisture. After you are sure they are completely dry, store the seeds in a packet made of an envelope or paper, clearly marked so that you can find them easily next season.

— PLANTING SEEDS IN EGGSHELLS —

When growing flower plants from seeds, start them in the halves of shells left over from hard-boiled eggs. When the time comes to transplant them, they can easily be removed by allowing the dirt in the shell to become hard and then breaking off the shell, whereupon the plant is placed in the ground. Or you can just crack the shells slightly and plant shell and seedling all at once—adding a nice little amendment to the soil.

A pasteboard box provided with holes large enough to support the eggshells can be used to hold them, unless egg cartons are at hand. Two large seeds such as nasturtiums and sweet peas can be planted in one shell, and four seeds of the smaller varieties.

— FUNNEL FOR WATERING PLANTS —

Slight results are obtained from watering plants in summer unless enough water is applied to reach the roots, which is particularly desirable with plants that have extensive root systems or long taproots. The funnel arrangement shown in the drawing is easily made and gets results with a minimum of water.

The funnel spout is perforated, as shown, and the lower end is provided with a point so that it may be easily thrust into the ground. In operation, the spout is pushed into the earth, close to the root of the plant to be watered, and the funnel is filled with water, which flows through the holes in the perforated spout. This serves not only to water the roots at the rate they drink but also to conserve

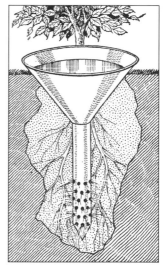

water over the operation of a sprinkler, which permits a great amount of evaporation.

— STARTING GARDEN PLANTS IN PAPER —

When starting small plants to get them ready to plant in the early spring, provide separate receptacles of paper; then the plant can be set out without trouble, and it will grow as if it had never been moved. Procure some heavy paper, and make the cups as shown.

The paper is cut into squares, the size depending on the plant, and each square is folded on the dotted line *AB*. This forms a triangle of double thickness. The next fold is made on the line *CD*, bringing the point *E* over to *F*. Then the paper is folded over on the line *FG*, bringing the point *H* over to *C*. This will leave a double-pointed end at *J*. The parts of this point are separated and folded down on the sides that form the cup, as shown.

These cups are filled with earth and set into earth placed in a box. The seeds are planted within the cups. When it comes time for transplanting, the cup with the plant is lifted out and set in the garden, without damage to the plant roots. The paper soon rots away and gives not trouble to the growing plant. The paper should have no ink on it, which could pollute the soil.

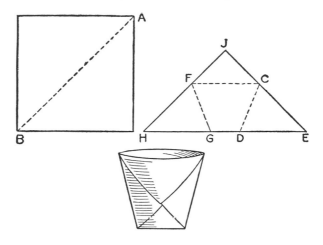

THE PAPER CUP STARTS ONE PLANT, AND WHEN RESET, NO DAMAGE RESULTS FROM THE CHANGE.

— CORNCOB "POTS" START PLANTS —

Small "pots" for starting plants without soil may be made from sections of dried corncobs. The seed is embedded in the center of the cob, and moisture is supplied by setting the cob in a shallow bowl of water. If desired, suitable chemicals can be added to the water to stimulate growth. The improvised pots are transplanted into the garden just as they are.

— EGGSHELLS AS FLOWERPOTS —

SEEDS WERE PLANTED IN THE EGGSHELLS, WHICH WERE BROKEN WITHOUT DISTURBING THE ROOTS WHEN TRANSPLANTED.

A novel method of caring for small plants until they are ready to be set out in the garden is shown above. Holes were bored in the bottom of the till of an old trunk and eggshells fitted into them. Seeds were planted in the shells, and the names of the varieties were marked on them. The arrangement is compact, and when the plants are ready for planting, the shells may be broken and the plants set without disturbing the roots.

— GROWING CLEAN STRAWBERRIES —

A very good method of growing individual strawberry plants that will produce large, clean berries is to provide a covering constructed from a board 10 in. square, with a 3-in. hole drilled in the center. This covering is placed over the plant, as shown in the sketch, to keep down weeds, retain moisture, and to make a base for the ripening berries. A shower cannot spatter dirt and sand on the growing fruit. The rays of the sun beating on the surface of the board will aid in ripening.

If a log can be obtained, the boards can be made better and more quickly.

GROWING STRAWBERRIES ON THE SURFACE OF A BOARD, WHERE THEY WILL RIPEN FAST AND KEEP CLEAN.

Disks about 1 in. thick are sawed from the log, and holes in their centers either cut with a chisel or drilled, as desired.

— CIGARETTE PAPERS KEEP CUTWORMS FROM DAMAGING TOMATOES —

You can protect newly set tomato plants against cutworm damage by wrapping the stalks with cigarette rolling papers or strips of newspaper. The paper should be twisted to hold it in

place and should project at least ½ in. above and below the ground. By the time the paper has rotted away, the plants will not be liable to cutworm damage.

— Young Trees Are Set in Sand to Prevent Disease —

By setting young fruit and shade trees in a bed of sand, one grower found that damage caused by insects and disease could be prevented. An excavation for the tree approximately 3 ft. in diameter and 8 in. deep is made, and just enough soil is placed around the roots to keep the tree standing. Then the hole is filled with sand. After the tree starts, it is watered until is has a firm foothold in the soil.

— Trunks of Young Trees Protected by Guards Cut from Garden Hose —

To protect the trunks of young trees from damage, one gardener made effective guards from lengths of garden hose that were wrapped around the trunks. He cut the hose spirally by placing it in a wooden channel and then rotating it while sawing at a 45-degree angle. No fastening was required because the tension of the hose held it firmly around the trunk.

— Proper Design for a Birdhouse —

If you enjoy the company of birds in your yard, you should make the yard inviting by providing suitable shelter. This birdhouse was designed and built to make a home for the American martin. The house will accommodate twenty families. All the holes are arranged so that they will not be open to the cold winds from the north, which often kill the

birds that come in the early spring. Around each opening is an extra ring of wood to make a longer passage, which assists the martin inside in fighting off the sparrow who tries to drive him out. The holes are made oval, to allow all the little ones to get their heads out for fresh air. The long overhanging eaves protect the little birds from the hot summer sun.

The rooms are made up with partitions on the inside; each opening will have a room. The inside of the rooms should be stained black.

— SPECIAL HANGERS PREVENT A SWING FROM DAMAGING A TREE —

Made so that there is no rubbing where it is fastened to the branch of a tree, this swing is sturdy enough for almost any child. The hangers are two lengths of flat iron that are bolted around the limb with pulleys attached to the hangers. The ropes are run through the sheaves and tied. There should be padding between the flat iron and the branch.

Whenever a swing of this sort is hung from a tree, you should first inspect that the tree has no rot and that it is mature and

strong. A large man should be able to hang from the branch chosen without the branch moving.

— Rocking Screen Sifts Dirt Quickly for Lawns and Small Gardens —

Having difficulty in sifting a couple loads of dirt with an ordinary screen sieve, a gardener made a rocking one in less than an hour. The device enabled him to do the job quickly. Scrap lumber was used to assemble the framework, and the legs were held in alignment at their top ends by means of corner braces. The screen was pivoted loosely to the legs, and the latter were pivoted to the base frame.

— Bee Feeder for Winter Use —

The use of a feeder, like that shown in the sketch, makes the feeding of bees in winter convenient. Syrup is fed to the bees from inverted glass jars, the openings of which are covered with muslin. The jars are encased in a packing of chaff in a wooden covering. The wooden box is made to fit over the hive, as shown in the sketch, and a 2-in. strip is nailed over the joint.

The device is made as follows: Use wood smoothed on both sides; pine, basswood, or other soft wood is satisfactory. Make two pieces, ⅞ in. thick, and the same size as the top of the

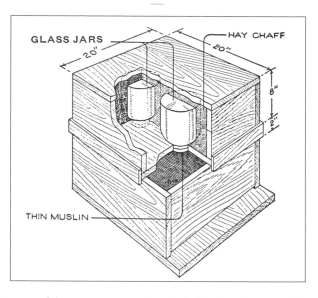

hive. Into one of these cut two round holes, as shown, to fit the necks of the jars. Make two pieces, 6¾ in. wide, for the sides, and two for the ends, the length being suited to the hive (the dimensions given in the sketch being suggestive only). Make four strips, 2 in. wide, and long enough to fit the four sides of the box. Nail the pieces of the box together as shown, nailing the sides over the endpieces and the top over the frame of the sides and ends. Pack chaff into the box, and, after filling the jars with syrup and covering their openings with muslin, pack the jars into the box so that their openings will be level with the bottom, through which

the holes have been cut. Fasten the board, with holes for the jars, into place with screws so that it may be removed when it is desired to remove the jars for refilling. Nail the 2-in. strips around the lower edge of the box so as to cover the joint between the box and the hive. The feeder is then fitted into place, the bees feeding from the surface of the muslin. The chaff prevents the syrup from congealing in cold weather so that it always available to the bees. The use of this simple device will prove economical and practical in keeping bees over the winter, assuring them a good food supply with little effort on the part of the keeper.

— A PRUNING-SAW GUARD —

THE TEETH ON THE UNUSED EDGE
ARE COVERED WITH A PIECE OF
BRASS CURTAIN ROD.

The double-edged pruning saw, with coarse teeth on one side and fine on the other, would be far more widely used if it were not for the fact that the unused edge so often injures the bark of the trunk when the saw is being used. A very satisfactory guard may be quickly made of a brass curtain rod by prying it apart slightly at the seam and cutting. A suitable length is cut to fit over the edge, as shown in the sketch. This will cling to the saw blade by its own tension.

— OLD WINDOW OR DOOR SCREEN USED AS FLOWER TRELLIS —

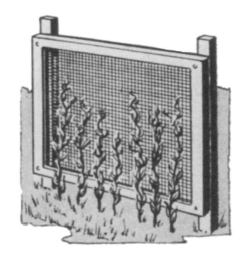

If you have a discarded window or door screen, it can be used as a trellis for sweet peas, morning glories, or other vines or climbing flowers. Just nail two stakes to the screen and anchor it as illustrated. The vines of the flowers will attach themselves to the screen wire strongly enough to avoid being blown down by an ordinary windstorm.

NATURAL *and* EASY PEST CONTROL

— HOW TO MAKE A TRAP FOR RABBITS, RATS, AND MICE —

You don't need to work hard to catch destructive rodents for release elsewhere—you just need a good trap. From an old 6-in. pine-fence board cut off four pieces, each 2½ ft. long; another, 6 in. square, for the end of the trap; and another, 4 x 8 in., for the door. Use old boards, because new boards will alert the rabbits that something is up.

Figure 1 shows how the box is made. It should be 4 in. wide by 6 in. high on the inside. The top and bottom boards project 1 in. beyond the side boards at the back, and the end board is set in. The top board should be 2 in. shorter than the sides at the front. Nail a strip on the top board, back of the door, and one on the bottom board so that the game cannot push the door open from inside the trap and get out.

In the middle of the top board, bore a hole and put a crotched stick in, on which the lever will rest. Bore another hole in the top of the door for

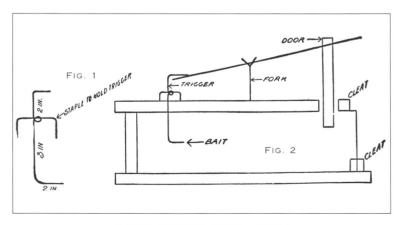

A GOOD TRAP FOR SMALL ANIMALS.

the lever to pass through. Bore a hole for the trigger 2 in. from the back of the box. The trigger must be made out of heavy ire (*Figure 2*). The door of the trap must work easily and loosely. Release the animals at least 2 mi. away, in a wooded area, to ensure that they don't find their way back.

— A NOVEL RAT TRAP —

A boy, while playing in the yard close to a grain house, dug a hole and buried an old-fashioned fruit jug that his mother had thrown away. The top part of the jug was left uncovered, as shown in the sketch, and a hole was broken in it just above the ground. The boy then placed some shelled corn in the bottom, put a board on top, and weighted it with a heavy stone.

The jug had been forgotten for several days when a farmer found it. Wondering what it was, he raised the board and found nine full-grown rats and four mice in the bottom.

The trap has since been in use for some time; it is opened every day or two and never fails to have from one to six rats or mice in it.

— A HOMEMADE RABBIT TRAP —

A good, serviceable rabbit trap can be made by sinking a common dry-goods box in the ground to within 6 in. of its top. A hole 6 or 7 in. square is cut in each end, level with the earth's surface. Boxes 18 in. long that will just fit are set in, hung on pivots with the longest end outside, so that they will lie horizontal. A rabbit may now look through the two tubes. The bait is hung on a string from the top of the large box so that it may be seen and smelled from the outside. The rabbit naturally goes into the holes, and in this trap there is nothing to awaken his suspicion. He smells the bait and squeezes along past the center

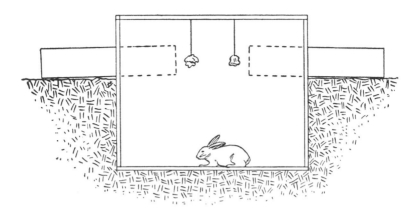

A RABBIT IN THE TRAP.

of the tube, when it tilts down and the game is shot into the pit. The tube rights itself at once for another catch. The top and sides of the large box may be covered with leaves, snow, or anything to hide it. A door placed in the top will enable the homeowner to remove the animals. By placing a little hay or other food in the bottom of the box, the trap need not be visited more often than once a week.

— ANTIDOTE FOR SQUIRREL PESTS —

To the owner of a garden where squirrels are protected by law, life in the summertime is a vexation. First the squirrels dig up the sweet corn, and two or three replantings are necessary. When the corn is within two or three days of being suitable for cooking, the squirrels come in droves from far and near. They eat all they can and carry away the rest. When the corn is gone, cucumbers, cabbages, etc., share the same fate, being partly eaten into. Even if you used a small target rifle morning and night, during your absence the devastation goes on steadily. The squirrels are often too wily for traps, and poison is far too dangerous to use. But it's easy to solve the problem. Shake cayenne pepper over the various vegetables that are being ruined and you'll soon have a peaceful garden.

— To Prevent Moles from Damaging Growing Seeds —

The foods most liked by the ground mole are the sprouts of peas and corn. A way to protect these growing seeds is to dip them in hot-pepper water (made by boiling chopped-up jalapeño peppers in a cup or two of water) just before planting. The mole will not touch the coated seeds, and the seeds are not injured in the least.

— A Good Mousetrap —

When opening a tomato or other small can, cut the cover crossways from side to side, making four triangular pieces in the top. Bend the four ends outward and remove the contents, wash clean, and dry; then bend the four ends inward, leaving a hole about ¾ in. in diameter in the center. Drop in a piece of bread and lay the can down upon its side, and the trap is set. The mouse can get in but cannot get out.

— Another Mousetrap —

A piece of an old bicycle tire and a glass fruit jar are the only materials required for making this trap. Push one end of the tire into the mousehole, making sure that there is a space left at the end so that the mouse can get in. Then bend the other end down into a fruit jar or other glass jar. Bait may be placed in the jar if desired, although

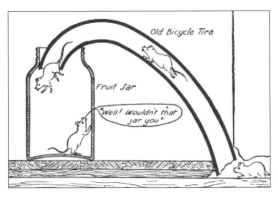

A BAITLESS TRAP.

this is not necessary for the trap to be effective.

— Destroying Caterpillars on Grapevines —

The grapes in one gardener's backyard were being destroyed by caterpillars, which could be found under all his grapevine's large leaves. The vine was almost dead when he initiated the following solution to his problem. He cut off all the large leaves, and those eaten by the caterpillars, which allowed the sun's rays to reach the grapes. This destroyed all the caterpillars, and the light and heat ripened the grapes.

— Dandelion Destroyer —

A lawn or yard thickly studded with dandelions presents a discouraging prospect at any time, but particularly when the owner considers digging them out. However, to a certain extent, the spread of the weeds can be controlled by preventing the blossoms from going to seed. The implement shown in the drawing, when pulled across a dandelion-infested lawn before the blossoms ripen, pulls off the flower heads, and thus effectively prevents self-seeding. A 12 x 16 in. piece of heavy galvanized iron, bent as shown, is toothed on one edge, the teeth being 1 in. apart and 1 in. deep. A piece of iron bar is riveted to the sheet iron so that it can be fastened to a handle and used in the same manner as a rake.

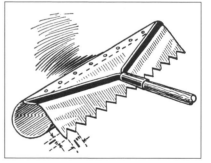

— Chemical-free Pest Control for the Garden —

Although there are a number of pesticides on the market—and many more you can make yourself— there are actually many wonderful natural ways to eliminate unwanted guests on your vegetation. Most just require a

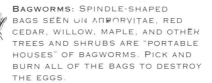

BAGWORMS: SPINDLE-SHAPED BAGS SEEN ON ARBORVITAE, RED CEDAR, WILLOW, MAPLE, AND OTHER TREES AND SHRUBS ARE "PORTABLE HOUSES" OF BAGWORMS. PICK AND BURN ALL OF THE BAGS TO DESTROY THE EGGS.

CUTWORMS: THESE WORMS WILL ATTACK YOUNG GARDEN PLANTS AND SOME ORNAMENTAL SEEDLINGS. TO CONTROL THEM, SCATTER A BRAN MUSH MADE FROM MIXING BRAN, WATER, AND COPIOUS CHILI POWDER AROUND THE PLANTS.

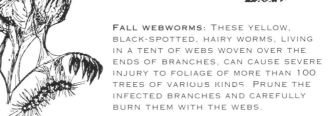

FALL WEBWORMS: THESE YELLOW, BLACK-SPOTTED, HAIRY WORMS, LIVING IN A TENT OF WEBS WOVEN OVER THE ENDS OF BRANCHES, CAN CAUSE SEVERE INJURY TO FOLIAGE OF MORE THAN 100 TREES OF VARIOUS KINDS. PRUNE THE INFECTED BRANCHES AND CAREFULLY BURN THEM WITH THE WEBS.

certain amount of effort; you do the work instead of some chemical.

The simplest strategy is to block access. To block the common cutworm, use cone-shaped paper disks over tender seedlings. Simple and effective, this solution can be easily instituted wherever this pest shows up.

You can also make tender leaves and shoots unappealing to insect invaders. Boil 1 qt. water with 1 tsp. pepper sauce or chili powder; let it sit until relatively cool; then pour the mixture into a spray bottle. Now spray liberally over all vulnerable plants. You'll find that pests large and small, from caterpillars to squirrels, will stay away from the fiery coated foliage. The application should be repeated every couple of weeks and after any rainfall.

Other solutions are offered in the sketches shown.

— Screen Wire Protects Small Trees against Damage by Rabbits —

If you have some screen wire available, especially some that is no longer serviceable for use on windows and doors, form it into sleeves to keep rabbits from gnawing the bark from young trees. Don't let your young saplings be killed or damaged by foraging wildlife.

The sleeves can be used year after year, and are much handier to put on and take off than cloth or paper, which are often used for the same purpose.

SCREEN WIRE

HOG RINGS

{ CHAPTER 2 }

DON'T REPLACE IT;
REPAIR IT!

— GAUNTLETS ON GLOVES —

When the fingers or palms of gloves with gauntlets wear out, do not throw away the gloves. Cut off the gauntlets and procure a pair of gloves with short wrists to which the old gauntlets can be sewn after the wristbands have been removed from the new gloves. The sewing may be done either by hand or on a machine, gathering in any fullness in the bellows of the cuff on the underside. A pair of gauntlets will outwear three or four pairs of gloves.

— REPAIRING CHRISTMAS-TREE DECORATIONS —

Small glass ornaments for Christmas-tree decorations are very easily broken on the line shown in the sketch. These can easily be repaired by inserting in the neck a piece of match, toothpick, or a splinter of wood and tying the hanging string to it.

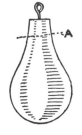

— How to Repair Linoleum —

A deep crack or fissure right in front of the kitchen cabinet spoiled the appearance of the new linoleum in one home. The damaged spot was removed with a sharp knife, and from a leftover scrap a piece was cut of the same outline and size. The edges were varnished, and then the patch was set in the open space. The linoleum was given a good coat of varnish, making it more durable. When perfectly dry, the new piece could not be detected.

— Substitute for a Broken Bench-vise Nut —

It is frequently the case that the nut on a bench-vise screw breaks from being subjected to a too-violent strain. If one is working in a place where a new nut cannot be obtained, the broken part may be replaced with the substitute shown in the sketch. Any piece of strap iron may be used. Using a round file and a drill, the two pieces can soon be made and attached to the bench with screws or bolts. A slight twist of the shaped

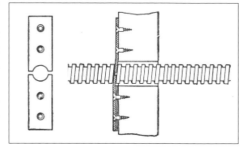

Pieces of strap iron shaped to fit the square thread make a good substitute nut.

ends is necessary to make them fit the angle of the thread.

— A Cheap, Quick, and Easy Fix for Damaged Marble —

With a little practice, any mechanic can repair holes, cracks, or chipped places on marble slabs so that the patched place cannot be distinguished from the natural marble. Use the following mixture as a base for the filler: water glass, 10 parts; calcined magnesite, 2 parts; and powdered marble, 4 parts. These should be mixed thoroughly to a semifluid paste. Fill the crack or hole, and smooth off level. Then use a camel's-hairbrush and colors made of aniline in alcohol to work out the veins, body colors, etc., as near to the natural marble as possible. It will depend on the application of the colors whether the repair can be seen or not. Artificial-marble slabs can be formed from this mixture.

— SHARPENING SCISSORS —

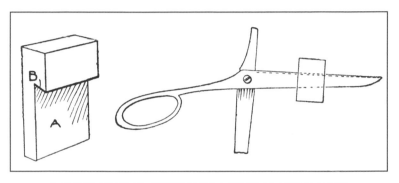

A BLOCK OF WOOD FITTED WITH A PIECE OF EMERY CLOTH FOR SHARPENING SCISSORS CORRECTLY.

When sharpening scissors on a grindstone it is very difficult to procure a straight edge. For those not having the facilities of a grinding arrangement, a very handy device that will produce a straight and sharp edge can be easily constructed as follows:

Procure a block of wood 1½ in. long, 1 in. wide, and ½ in. thick. Saw a kerf square with the face of the block, as shown at *A*. Glue a piece of fine emery cloth in the kerf, at *B*, taking care to lay it flat on the sloping surface only, and allowing no part of the cloth to turn the sharp corner and lie on the back. Apply the block to the scissor blade as shown, and draw it back and forth from one end to the other. Be careful to keep the back of the blade flat against the block. Anyone can sharpen scissors correctly with this block, without being familiar with scissors grinding.

— SHAPING AN OLD BROOM —

METHOD OF STRAIGHTENING A BROOM'S STRAWS.

A broom having the straws bent and out of shape, yet not worn out, can be fixed up like new in the following manner: Slightly dampen the straw with water, and wrap with heavy paper. Then place a weight on the flat portion of the broom. After standing under pressure for several days the straw will be restored to the shape of a new broom. Paintbrushes can be treated in the same manner; but in that case the bristles of the paintbrush should be slightly moistened with linseed oil rather than water.

— REPAIRING ROCKERS ON A CHAIR —

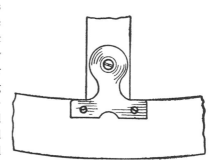

When the tenons on the posts of a rocking chair were broken off so close to the rocker that it was impossible to make ordinary repairs, four window-shade roller brackets were used in the following manner: The metal was straightened so that it would lie flat, and two brackets were used on the end of each post. This made a neat and strong repair.

— TO REPAIR A LEAK IN A CANOE —

After striking some rocks with a canoe, it sprung three very bad leaks. These were effectively patched with pieces of cheesecloth, well soaked in liquid shellac, which were pasted on the outside of the leak. After allowing this to set for a few hours, it will be almost impossible to remove the patch. This is an inexpensive and almost invariably a sure remedy for leaks. When the cloth is dry, paint it over with the same color as the boat, and the repair can scarcely be seen.

— REPAIR FOR A BROKEN LOCK KEEPER —

Having broken the recess of a common cupboard lock, or latch, which was used to fasten a hinged storm window, a homeowner used a round-headed wood screw, as shown. The screw was easily placed, and it serves the purpose as well as the regular keeper.

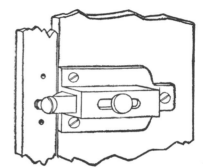

— REPAIRING A WORN STOPCOCK —

The plug of a worn stopcock of the type shown in the illustration, or one that has been reground, will project beyond the bottom. This creates a problem, because the ring, or washer, and screw will not draw it tightly into place.

To remedy this trouble, file off a portion of the plug on the line *AA* and file off a sufficient amount of the screw on the line *BB*. When the plug is replaced and the washer and screw drawn up, the stopcock will be as good as new.

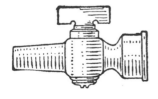
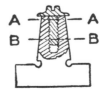

REMOVING A PORTION OF THE PLUG AND SHORTENING THE SCREW ALLOWS THE PARTS TO BE DRAWN TIGHTLY TOGETHER

— NEEDLE FOR REPAIRING SCREENS —

In attaching patches to window or door screens, the work requires a continual shifting from one side to the other. Or, two persons, one on each side, must be present to pass the threaded needle back and forth. The operation can be easily simplified by using a bent needle that has been heated and suitably shaped. The point of this needle can always be made to return to the side from which it entered, thereby avoiding the need for an assistant or the tiresome shifting back and forth.

— REPAIRING A BROKEN KNIFE HANDLE —

A piece was broken from the pearl handle of a hunter's knife. He repaired it as follows: After cleaning both the edges of the pearl and the brass beneath, he ran in enough solder to fill the place of the piece of pearl broken out. The solder was then filed, sandpapered, and polished.

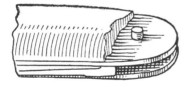 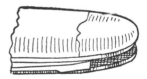

KNIFE REPAIR WITH SOLDER.

— REPAIRING A BROKEN OILSTONE —

A broken oilstone can be repaired and made as good as new in the following manner: Warm the pieces by heating them on the top of a stove or gas heater with a piece of heavy sheet metal placed on it so as to protect the stone from the direct heat of the flame. The heating should be done slowly, or the stone will crack.

When the stone is warm, wipe off the oil that the heat has driven out, and apply a couple of coats of shellac to the broken ends. When the shellac is thoroughly dry, warm the stone again to melt the shellac, and clamp the pieces together. After cooling, the pieces will be found firmly stuck together.

— Scissors Sharpener —

Procure an ordinary wood clothespin and drill an ⅛-in. hole through its blades. Then insert a piece of hardened ⅛-in. drill rod, which should be a driving fit. In using this device, take the scissors and attempt to cut the steel rod. Do this three or four times, and a good cutting edge will be obtained.

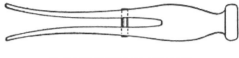

IN ATTEMPTING TO CUT THE HARDENED STEEL PIN, THE EDGE IS DRAWN SHARP.

— How to Mend Shoes —

Everybody wears out shoes, and by the same token, everybody ought to know how to mend them. The statement that shoe profits are "paper" profits only serves to confirm a lurking suspicion that paper is involved somewhere, a suspicion first engendered by the rapidity with which many shoes wear out. Cobbling is not high art, but it is good economy, and he who has a pair of old shoes that can be renovated by straightening up the heels and adding new taps, or half soles, and does these things, contributes his bit toward reducing the cost of living and the amount of waste in our landfills.

An outfit of shoe-repairing tools and materials is simple and inexpensive, and can usually be purchased for less than the price of a set of soles.

Before proceeding with the actual work, it is wise for the "cobbler" to familiarize himself with the various parts of a shoe, as shown in the small drawing, after which he is prepared to tackle a job of half-soling.

First the shoes are set on the leather, and the new taps are marked out and cut a trifle larger than the old sole. These pieces are soaked for a few minutes in warm water, to soften the leather. While the leather is thus "mellowing," the old sole is removed, as in *Figure 1*. Cut the thread with a knife if the soles are sewed on and, if the shoes have never been resoled, the worn sole is cut off at the shank, as in *Figure 2*, paring the shank down to a thin taper, or scarf, to make a neat splice with the new sole, which should be similarly

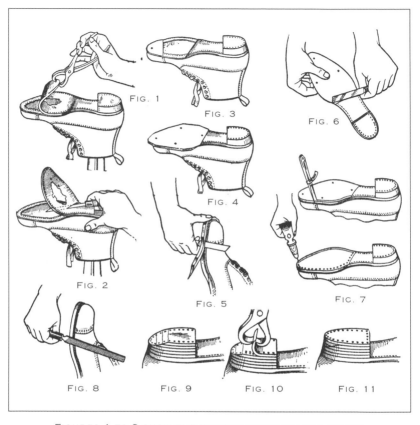

FIG. 1

FIG. 3

FIG. 6

FIG. 4

FIG. 2

FIG. 5

FIG. 7

FIG. 8

FIG. 9

FIG. 10

FIG. 11

FIGURES 1 TO 8 SHOW THE VARIOUS STEPS IN HALF-SOLING
A SHOE, AND FIGURES 9 TO 11 SHOW HOW
WORN HEELS ARE REPAIRED.

scarfed. The leather is removed from the water and pounded on the last, evenly and thoroughly, with the hammer, to "harden" it. The shoe is then placed on the last, and a piece of shoemakers' tarred felt, half the length and width of the sole, is placed under the sole to prevent squeaking. If the toe of the shoe has been worn down so that the welt is not in good condition, a tapering piece of leather is tacked to the toe to build

it up, as in *Figure 3.*
The sole is fastened
in place with four
nails, as shown in
Figure 4. In nailing,
the pegging awl is
used to the start the
nail. The hole is not
made too deep, just
deep enough to hold
the nail in position.
The nails are not
driven perpendicu-
larly but with a slight

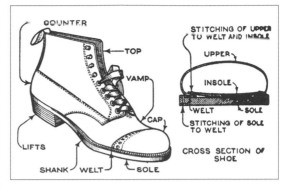

A STUDY OF THE COMPONENT PARTS OF THE SHOE
IS SUGGESTED BEFORE STARTING TO WORK.

slant toward the center, to hold the sole more securely.

After the sole has been tacked to the shoe as shown, the surplus leather around the edge is trimmed away, as in *Figure 5,* so that it will be approximately flush with the sole; this is necessary so that the repairman will have an approximately correct outline to work from in order to get the nails in evenly. *Figure 6* shows how the tap should be pared, or scarfed down, at the shank to make a neat joint at the point where the new sole laps over and joins the old one.

A line is scribed with a compass, or by other means, as indicated in *Figure 7,* at a point from ¼ to ½ in. from the edge of the sole. This depends upon the size of the shoe and the width of the welt beyond the

upper. Then awl holes are made at ½ -in. intervals along the line, and the nails are driven in. Be sure the nails strike the last and clinch, and pound the heads down flush with the surface. If any nails bend over, withdraw them and put in new ones. Allow the leather to dry slowly, and then finish off the edge of the sole with a rasp or a piece of broken window glass, which makes a good scraper. If a finer finish is desired, sandpaper can be used. After the soles have been finished, the raw edges are coated with shoe polish to correspond with the color of the shoe.

Normally most persons wear the heel off at the back, as shown in *Figure 9,* but others walk so that the heel runs over at either side. In such cases the worn top pieces, or lifts, as they are called, are removed, as in *Figure 10,* and the projecting nails or pegs pulled out. Then the heels may be built up of tapered pieces in the same manner as described for repairing a worn toe. These pieces serve to use up the odds and ends of leather. The small wedge-shaped pieces are tacked to the heel, and the bottom lift is applied in exactly the same manner as the sole, the finished job appearing as in *Figure 11.* Of course, there is no objection to removing all the worn lifts and replacing them with new ones, if leather is available.

Before the mended shoe is ready for wear, it is wise to go over the nail heads with a file to take off any slight projections; examine the inside for nails, and pound down thoroughly any projecting points or prominent clinches. A lining of thin leather cemented over the insole is desirable, especially at the heel.

Anybody can learn to do a good job of shoe repairing in a short time, and even if one is not naturally "handy with tools" but uses care in nailing and cutting, the first attempt will generally be surprisingly good.

— FASTEN LOOSE TABLE LEGS —

When legs of an ordinary table become loose and unsteady they may be easily repaired as shown in the sketch. Nails do not hold well in such places, and glue will not stand much washing. The method of making the repair is to drill ⅛-in. holes through the rails on each side of the leg and insert pieces of galvanized wire of a size to fit the holes. After the wire is inserted, the ends are bent over. The illustration clearly shows the repair.

A PIECE OF WIRE BENT AROUND THE LEG OF A TABLE WILL MAKE IT RIGID.

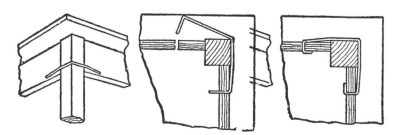

— MATCH GETS BALLPOINT GOING —

Squeeze extra mileage out of your ballpoint pens with an occasional hotfoot. Most pens clog and stop writing long before their ink runs dry. In this case, the heat from a single match often will start the flow again. Be careful to only heat the tip; do not melt the body of the pen in the flame.

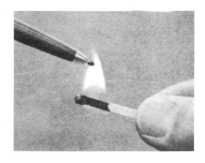

— HOW TO CANE CHAIRS —

There are but few households that do not have at least one or two chairs without a seat or back. The same households may have someone who would enjoy recaning the chairs if he only knew how to do it. He could also make considerable pin money by repairing chairs for the neighbors. If the following directions are carried out, new cane seats and backs can easily be put on chairs where they are broken or sagged to an uncomfortable position.

The first thing to do is to remove the old cane. This can be done by turning the chair upside down and, with the aid of a sharp knife or chisel, cutting the cane between the holes. After this is done, the old bottom can be pulled out. If plugs are found in any of the holes, they should be knocked out. If the beginner is in doubt about finding which holes along any curved sides should be used for the cane running nearly parallel to the edge, he may find it to his advantage to mark the holes on the underside of the frame before removing the old cane.

The worker should be provided with a small sample of the old cane. A bundle of similar material may be secured at any first-class hardware store.

The cane usually comes in lengths of about 15 ft., and each bundle contains enough to reseat several chairs. In addition to the cane, the worker should provide himself with a piece of bacon rind; a square pointed wedge, as shown in *Figure 1;* and 8 or 10 round wood plugs. These are used for temporarily holding the ends of the cane in the holes.

Untie one of the strands that has been well soaked. Put it about 3 to 4 in. down through the hole at one end of what is to be the outside strand of one side, and secure it in this hole by means of one of the small plugs mentioned. The plug should not be forced in too hard nor cut off, because it must be removed again. The other end of the strand should be made pointed and passed down through the hole at the opposite side and, after having been pulled tight, held there by inserting another plug.

Pass the end up through the next hole, then across

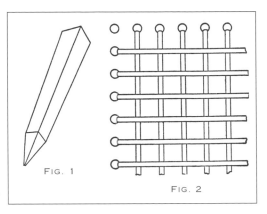

FIG. 1
FIG. 2

FIRST LAYER OF STRANDS.

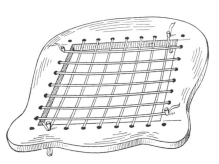

FIRST TWO LAYERS IN PLACE.

and down, and hold it while the second plug is moved to the last hole through which the cane was drawn. Proceed across the chair bottom in the same manner. Whenever the end of one strand is reached, it should be held by a plug and a new one started in the next hole, as in the beginning. No plugs should be permanently removed until another strand of cane is through the same hole to hold the first strand in place. After laying the strands across the seat in one direction, put in another layer at right angles and lying entirely above the first layer. Both of these layers when in place appear as shown in the illustration above.

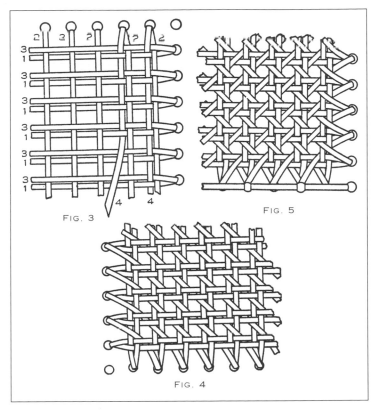

FIG. 3

FIG. 5

FIG. 4

THREE STAGES OF WEAVING.

After completing the second layer, stretch the third one, using the same holes as for the first layer. This will make three layers, the first being hidden by the third, while the second layer is at right angles to and between the first and third. No weaving has been done up to this time, nothing but stretching and threading the cane through the holes. The cane will have the appearance shown in *Figure 3*. The next thing to do is to start the cane across in the same direction as the second layer and begin the weaving. The top or third layer strands should be pushed toward the end from which the weaving starts so that the strand being woven may be pushed down between the first and third layers, and up again between pairs. The two first strands of the fourth layer are shown woven in *Figure 3*. During the weaving, the strands should be lubricated with the rind of bacon to make them pass through with ease. Even with this lubrication, one can seldom weave more than halfway across the seat with the pointed end before finding it advisable to pull the remainder of the strand through. After finishing this fourth layer of strands, it is quite probable that each strand will be about midway between its two neighbors, instead of lying close to its mate as desired. Here is where the square and pointed wedge is used. The wedge is driven down between the proper strands to move them into place.

Start at one corner and weave diagonally, as shown in *Figure 4*, making sure that the strand will slip in between the two that form the corner of the square in each case. One more weave across, on the diagonal, and the seat will be finished, except for the binding, as shown in *Figure 5*. The binding consists of one strand that covers the row of holes while it is held down with another strand, a loop over the first being made every second or third hole, as desired. It will be of great assistance to keep another chair with a cane bottom at hand to examine while recaning the first chair.

— TIGHTENING CANE IN FURNITURE —

Split cane, used as part of furniture such as chair seats, often becomes loose, and the threads of cane pull out. This can be prevented by sponging with hot water or by applying steaming cloths to the cane. This process also tightens the shreds of cane, and it does not injure ordinary furniture. If the article is highly polished, care should be taken to prevent the hot water from coming in contact with anything but the cane.

— 🦎🦎🦎 —

{ CHAPTER 3 }

HOME ECONOMICS

NATURAL CLEANING

— CLEANING CEILINGS NATURALLY —

To clean smoke, dirt, grease, fly specks, etc., from a painted ceiling or wall, make a mixture of vinegar, baking soda, and a little table salt, and rub the grimed surface with it. Follow by washing off with warm water and soap, and wipe dry using a soft rag. This method is also good for enameled baths, glass, and white porcelain.

— CLEAN PAINTED OR FRESCOED WALLS —

Use a paste made of vinegar and baking soda with a small amount of salt added. The ingredients should be mixed in a large dish and applied to the wall with a cloth. The grease and fly specks as well as the carbon deposits from kitchen smoke are quickly removed. The mixture is harmless. After the wall is thoroughly cleaned, it should be washed with warm water and soap, and then dried with a cloth. The mixture works equally well on enameled baths and glass or white porcelain.

— STARCH SOLUTION CLEANS WOODWORK —

Woodwork in your kitchen that has become stained from smoke and grease can be cleaned by painting it with a solution of starch in water. After the solution has dried, it is rubbed off with a soft brush or clean cloth, which removes the stains. Treating the woodwork in this way does not harm the paint, and any finished surface treated with starch will remain in good condition for several years.

— CORNER CLEANER ATTACHED TO A SCRUBBING BRUSH —

Dirt will accumulate and harden in the corners of a floor and baseboard just because the end of a scrubbing brush will not enter them. The water gets in with the dirt and leaves a hard crust. This may be easily cleaned out if a metal point is attached to the end of the brush handle, as shown in the illustration. The point is used as a scraper to break up the crust and clean it out where the bristles will not enter.

— INEXPENSIVE WALLPAPER CLEANER —

Add about 2 oz. ammonia to 1 qt. flour and enough luke-warm water to make a dough. Wipe the paper with it while turning and kneading it, as in making dough. This will take up the dirt, and a clean side is always presented to the paper. Use only in a well-ventilated area, and be sure to remove any dough from the wallpaper when you are done.

— WALLPAPER CLEANER —

This cleaner is only to be used on coated papers, not on uncoated or delicate papers. Make a small quantity by combining 1½ c. water with ½ c. salt in a pan, heating it just to the point of boiling (about 180°F). Remove the pan from the stove and add 1 tb. tetrachloride (or have an adult add 1 tb. kerosene), 2 tb. alum, and 3 c. good grade bread flour. Stir quickly to prevent lumps; continue stirring until a thick paste forms. Knead the dough until it is smooth and not sticky. It may be necessary to use a little less flour, since flours differ in starch content. Apply a small ball of dough to the soiled wallpaper with even strokes, working downward. Discard the dough when it becomes soiled.

— A FELT-PAD SILVER CLEANER —

One of the most effective methods of cleaning silver is to use a felt-covered block. Several layers of felt are stretched over a block of wood about 2 x 4 x 6 in. and tacked at the ends. A quantity of whiting is then rubbed into the felt, and the pad is moistened with ammonia before using. Used in the same manner as the old-style scouring brick, the results are much more satisfactory. It will not be necessary to renew the whiting frequently, but a few drops of ammonia added each time it is used is advised.

— A CLEANER FOR BRASS —

In some recent laboratory experiments the following solution was found to cleanse brass very quickly without harm to the hands or the metal. An ounce of alum was put into a pint of boiling water and the solution rubbed on the brass with a cloth. Stains as well as tarnish were quickly removed. The solution is inexpensive and easily prepared.

— NATURAL WAY TO CLEAN AND POLISH SHOES —

In using the polishes now on the market for tans [shoes], one man found that the leather cracked in an unreasonably short time. The following was suggested and tried out with good results: Wash the shoes with castile soap and water by applying the mixture with a dauber. Work up a little lather, and then rub dry with a cloth, without rinsing. The leather will be cleaned without becoming dark, and it will not crack. A higher polish may be obtained by using some paste polish in the usual manner.

— CHEAP AND NATURAL FURNITURE POLISH —

A good, pastelike furniture polish that is very cheap and keeps indefinitely can be made as follows: Mix 3 oz. white wax, 2 oz. pearl ash (commonly known as potassium carbonate), and 6 oz. water. Heat the mixture until it becomes dissolved, then add 4 oz. boiled linseed oil. Stir well and pour into cans to cool. Apply with a cloth and rub to a polish.

— OIL SOLUTIONS FOR CLEANING —

This is for ordinary dusting of nonwaxed wood or metal surfaces. Put 1 tb. paraffin, lemon, or boiled linseed oil into a quart jar, cover, and turn the jar until the oil is spread evenly over the inner surface of jar. Put a dust cloth in the jar and leave overnight. The oil will be evenly distributed on the cloth.

Do not use any formula containing boiled linseed in proximity to an open flame.

— STEAM CLEANING BATHROOM WALLS —

Sometimes the simplest solutions are the best. Painted bathroom walls often can be cleaned by filling the tub with very hot water and letting the room steam for about five minutes, after which the walls and ceiling can be wiped clean with a dry cloth.

— USING ELECTROLYSIS FOR CLEANING SILVER —

To make your silver as bright as new, use the following labor-saving solution:

Combine 1 qt. boiling water to 1 tsp. baking soda, 1 tsp. salt, and 1 sheet of aluminum foil, in a large kettle. If necessary, double or triple the recipe to completely immerse the silver, which must be in contact with the sheet of aluminum foil. Keep the water at the boiling point throughout the cleaning process. Remove and wash the cleaned silver in hot, soapy water; rinse and polish with a soft, dry cloth. A clean, inexpensive aluminum kettle may be used in place of an enamel kettle and the sheet of aluminum foil. Because aluminum deteriorates somewhat in the cleaning solution, valuable utensils should not be used. Pour out the cleaning solution as soon as the silver is removed.

— CLEANING LEATHER ON FURNITURE —

Carefully beat the whites of three eggs, and use a piece of flannel to rub the whites well into the leather, which will become clean and lustrous. For black leathers, some lampblack may be added and the mixture applied in the same way.

— A TASTY AND EFFECTIVE FURNITURE POLISH —

Boiled olive oil to which a few drops of vinegar has been added makes an excellent furniture polish for very fine woods. It will be found to work nicely on highly polished surfaces, and also works well for automobile bodies. It is applied in moderate quantities and rubbed to a luster with a clean flannel cloth.

— CLEANING RUBBER GOODS —

Ordinary soap and water is usually not sufficient to take dirt off the surface of soft-rubber goods—for instance, oily stains on tires. Nor are abrasive cleaners much better. Crystals of trisodium phosphate sprinkled on a wet brush and scrubbed vigorously on the rubber act quickly as a cleansing agent. Plenty of water should be used, and the crystals must be carefully washed off of the rubber after it is clean.

— MOTHER NATURE'S CLEANER FOR CANVAS SHOES —

One of the most economical cleansers for canvas shoes is oxide of zinc. Mix a small quantity of the powder with water, to the consistency of thin paste. Then apply it to the canvas with an old toothbrush, rubbing it in thoroughly. Let the shoes dry before wearing them.

— Removing Tarnish —

A pencil eraser will remove the tarnish from nickel plate, and an ink eraser will remove the rust from drawing instruments.

— Cleaning Burnt Pans —

Boiling soda water in burnt pans is often advocated, but, although this method seems to be successful in removing the burnt food, it makes the pans apt to burn again. A better method is to fill the pans with a saturated solution of salt and water, letting the solution stand overnight. Then put the pan on the flame and bring the water to a boil, which will cause the burnt particles to loosen so that they can be easily removed.

Kitchen Shortcuts

Vegetable Slicer

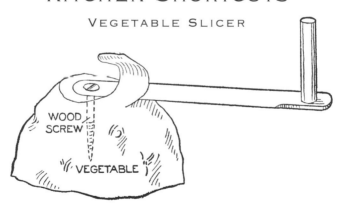

SLICER IN VEGETABLE.

Endlessly slicing vegetables for stews, salads, and other dishes is one of the most tedious labors a home cook must endure. This slicer makes the process somewhat easier. It is made of a knife blade, screw, and pin handle. The screw is soldered into the end of the knife blade. As the screw feeds into the vegetable or fruit, the blade will slice it in a curl of even thickness.

— TABLESPOON END USED AS LEMON SQUEEZER —

In an emergency, the ordinary tablespoon can be used as a lemon squeezer, by turning the lemon around the end of the spoon. This produces the same result as obtained with the regular squeezers, which act on the principle of extracting the juice by turning and crushing the lemon over a rough projection that approximately matches the shape of a half lemon.

THE SHAPE OF THE SPOON BOWL PRODUCES THE SAME EFFECT AS THE LEMON SQUEEZER.

AN EGGSHELL FUNNEL

Bottles having small necks are hard to fill without spilling the liquid inside. A funnel cannot be used in a small opening, and pouring with a graduate glass requires a steady hand. When you do not have a graduate at hand, a half eggshell with a small hole pricked in the end will serve better than a funnel. Place the shell in an oven to brown the surface slightly and it will be less brittle and last much longer.

A CHERRY SEEDER

HAIRPIN IN STICK.

An ordinary hairpin is driven partway into a small, round piece of wood about ⅜ in. in diameter and 2 or 2½ in. long, for a handle, as shown in the sketch. The hairpin should be a very small size. To operate, simply insert the wire loop into the cherry where the stem has been pulled off and lift out the seed.

— PREVENTING VEGETABLES FROM BURNING IN A POT —

Many housekeepers do not know that there is a clever yet simple way to prevent potatoes from burning and sticking to the bottom of a pot. An inverted pie pan placed in the bottom of the pot avoids scorching potatoes. The water and empty space beneath the pie pan saves the potatoes. This trick also makes the work of cleaning pots easier, as no adhering parts of potatoes are left to be scoured out.

— STEEL WOOL AS ALUMINUMWARE CLEANER —

It takes little trouble to keep aluminum pots and pans shining if they are cleaned frequently with steel wool, water, and nonalkaline soap. Use a very fine grade of the steel wool, and give the pots and pans a few rubs frequently rather than attempting to clean them only occasionally, after they have accumulated much soil.

KITCHEN CHOPPING-BOARD AID

Cooks can slice, chop, or mince vegetables and various other foods rapidly by placing the little device shown here on a chopping board. It is an ordinary staple, driven in just far enough to allow a space for the end of a pointed kitchen knife to fit in it. The staple is driven into the edge of the chopping board. The knife can be raised and lowered with one hand as the material

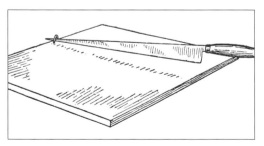

KNIFE ATTACHED TO THE BOARD.

is passed under the blade with the other. Great pressure can be applied and the knife will not slip.

— A Time-saving Baking Pan —

When making cookies, tarts, or similar pastry, the housewife often wishes for something by which to lift the baked articles from the pan. The baking tray or pan shown in the sketch not only protects the hands from burns but also allows the baked articles to easily be slipped from its surface. The pan is made from a piece of sheet iron

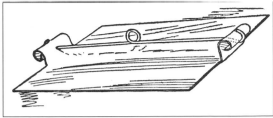

BAKING PAN WITHOUT SIDES.

slightly larger than the baking space desired. Each end of the metal is cut so that a part may be turned up and formed into a roll to make handles for the pan.

— Aid in Mixing Salad Dressing —

Some cooks find it a very difficult matter to prepare salad dressing, principally mayonnaise dressing, as the constant stirring and pouring of oil and liquids are required in the operation. The simple homemade device shown in the accompanying sketch greatly assists in this work. It consists of a stand to hold a bottle, the mouth of which rests against a small gate, directly in the rear of the attached tin trough. The weight of the bottle and the

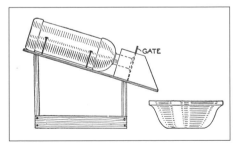

BOTTLE IN STAND

contents against the gate serves as a check or stopper. If the gate is raised slightly, it will permit a continuous flow of liquid of the desired amount.

— ALUMINUM FOIL SPEEDS IRONING —

Spreading a sheet of aluminum foil over the ironing-board pad before tying down the cover speeds ironing considerably. The metal keeps the moisture in sprinkled clothes and reflects heat from the iron, and thus helps to produce steam. Be careful to test this with delicates before ironing.

— DEVICE QUARTERS AND CORES APPLES AND OTHER FRUIT —

The arrangement shown in the sketch was made to provide a simple homemade device for cutting apples and other fruit into quarters and at the same time removing the core. The circular frame is built up

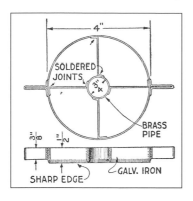

around a ring, ¾ in. in diameter, and the ribs and handles are soldered to it. A strip of galvanized iron, ½ in. wide, was used for the cutting portion, and the lower edge was filed sharp and then finished with a small oilstone. In use, the cutter is set over the fruit, as shown, and by pressure on the handles, the fruit is cut neatly.

— A FRUIT STEMMER —

The stemmer shown in the sketch is a very handy article for the kitchen during berry season. It is made of spring steel, and tempered,

the length being about 2½ in. The end used for removing the stem is ground from the outside edge after tempering.

A ring large enough to admit the second finger is soldered at a convenient distance from the end on one leg.

— KITCHEN-UTENSIL SCRAPER —

A flexible utensil scraper is one of the most useful articles to have in the kitchen. It covers such a large surface in scraping pans, kettles, etc., that this most disagreeable part of the kitchen work is quickly and easily accomplished.

The flexible blade is attached to the tin handles with small rivets. The blade should be thin and narrow enough to allow it to bend. When the handles are pressed together, the blade curves to the shape of the given utensil's surface.

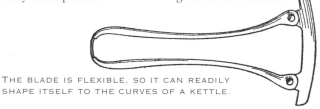

THE BLADE IS FLEXIBLE, SO IT CAN READILY SHAPE ITSELF TO THE CURVES OF A KETTLE.

— A FRUIT-JAR OPENER —

The accompanying sketch shows a handy device for turning and unscrewing the covers on glass fruit jars. The loop is slipped over the cover and the handle turned in the direction of the arrow. To unscrew the cover, the tool is turned over and the handle turned in the opposite direction. The

loop should be just large enough to slip over the cover easily.

It is made of leather and fastened to the wood handle with screws.

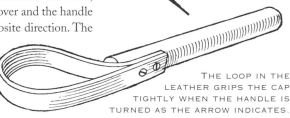

THE LOOP IN THE LEATHER GRIPS THE CAP TIGHTLY WHEN THE HANDLE IS TURNED AS THE ARROW INDICATES.

— A Cover Strainer —

Quite frequently the cook or housewife wishes to pour the hot water or liquid from boiling vegetables or other foods without removing the solids from the kettle. This is easily accomplished if small holes are drilled in the cover, as shown in the sketch. The saucepan or kettle can be tilted, and the liquid drains through the holes. Further, the steam from cooking food can readily

A SUFFICIENT NUMBER OF HOLES ARE DRILLED IN THE EDGE OF THE COVER TO MAKE A STRAINER.

escape through the holes, thus preventing the cover from vibrating or the liquids from boiling over. Better safe than sorry!

— Kitchen-knife Sharpener —

A good, serviceable knife sharpener may be made from a piece of steel cut as shown, with two screw holes drilled for fastening it to a piece of wood or to a table. The knife is drawn through and sharpened on either side. Both positions of the knife are shown. The steel is hardened before fastening it in place.

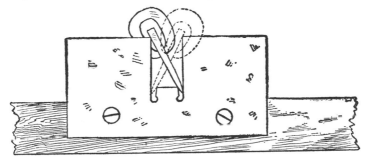

SHARPENER ON TABLE EDGE.

Stretching Resources

— To Longer Preserve Cut Flowers —

A good way to keep cut flowers fresh is to place a small amount of pure salt in the water. It is best to procure this salt at a drugstore, because commercial salt will cause the flowers to wither, due to the impurities in the soda. Call for pure sodium chloride.

— How to Make a Candle Shade —

PUNCHING THE HOLES.

Lay out the pattern for the shade on a thin piece of paper, 9 x 12 in., making the arcs of the circle with a pencil compass. As shown in the sketch, the pattern for this particular shade covers a half circle, with 2¾ in. added. Allowance must be made for the lap, and because ¼ in. will do, a line is drawn parallel ¼ in. from the one drawn through the center to the outside circle that terminates the design.

Nail a thin sheet of brass, about 9 in. wide by 12 in. long, to a smooth board of soft wood. Then trace the design on the brass by laying a piece of carbon paper between the pattern and the brass. After transferring the design to the brass, use a small awl to punch the holes in the brass, along the outlines of the figures traced. Punch holes in the brass in the spaces around the outlined figures, excepting the ¼ in. around the outside of the pattern. When all the holes are punched, remove the brass sheet from the board, and cut it along the outer lines as traced from the pattern, then bend the brass carefully so as not to crease the figures appearing in relief. When the edges are brought together by bending, fasten them with brass-headed nails or brads.

If a wood-turning lathe is at hand, the shade can be made better by turning a cone from soft wood that will fit the sheet-brass shade after it is shaped, allowing the edges to be fastened together. The pattern is traced as before. But before punching the holes, cut out the brass on the outside lines, bend into shape, fasten the ends together, and place on the wood cone. The holes are now punched on the outlines traced from the pattern, and the open spaces made full of holes. With the holes being punched after the shade is shaped, the metal will stay and hold the perfect shape of a cone much better.

The glass-beaded fringe is attached on the inside of the bottom part with small brass rivets or brads, placed about ¾ in. apart. The thin-sheet brass may be procured from the local hardware dealer and sometimes can be purchased from general merchandise stores.

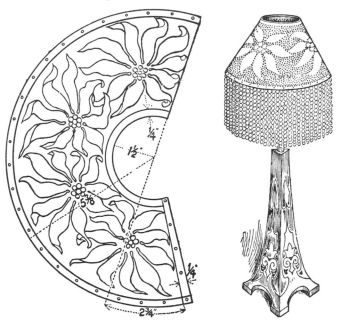

LEFT: COMPLETED SHADE PATTERN. RIGHT: THE COMPLETED SHADE.

— How to Make a Trousers Hanger —

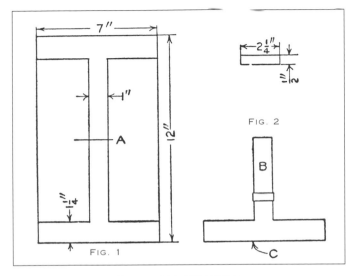

CUT FROM SHEET METAL.

Secure a piece of sheet metal 7 in. wide and 12 in. long. Cut the metal as shown in *Figure 1*, and make a close bend at point *A*, but not too close to cause it to break. The piece will then appear as shown in *Figure 2*. Cut a piece from the waste material ½ in. wide and 2¼ in. long, and bend it around the two pieces *B*, *Figure 2*, so that it will slide freely on their length. Bend in the edges, *C*, ⅛ in. to hold the trousers firmly. Drill a hole through the top end of *B*, and attach a wire formed into a hook for use in hanging on a nail. The bottom ends of the trousers are inserted between the jaws, *C*, and the small ferrule pushed to clamp them on the cloth.

— Preserving Paint in Open Cans —

To keep paint from drying out in an open can, it is necessary to exclude the air from the oil. This can be done by procuring a paper sack that's been tested for airtightness by blowing into it. Set the can into the sack, and tie it tightly with a cord. Mixed paint will be kept in a working state in this manner.

Save the brushes you've used in this paint as well. Wrap them tightly in plastic wrap so that no air remains around the brush, and store the brush in the freezer. Next time you need to use it, merely pull it out, let it warm up, and you're good to go!

— THAWING OUT FROZEN PIPES —

When the water pipes connecting a range boiler become frozen, get a plumber and avoid an explosion of the water back. If, however, the frozen pipe is a cold-water pipe in no way connected with the hot-water boiler, it can be thawed out as follows:

Procure some grain alcohol—not denatured or wood alcohol—and, after turning the spigot upward or upside down, as shown, open it and pour in the alcohol.

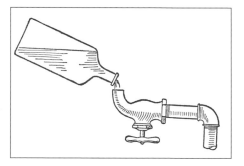

THE FAUCET IS TURNED UPWARD AND OPENED, AND ALCOHOL POURED IN ON THE ICE.

When the water begins to flow, turn it to its proper position.

— HOMEMADE FLOOR POLISHER —

A floor polisher is something that one does not use but two or three times a year. Thus, most homeowners are reluctant to buy one. Manufactured polishers come in two sizes, one weighing 15 lb., which is the right size for family use, and one weighing 25 lb.

A polisher can be made at home that will do the work just as well. Procure a wooden box such as cocoa tins or starch packages are shipped in, and stretch several thicknesses of flannel or carpet over the bottom. Allow the edges to extend well up the sides, and tack smoothly. Make a handle of two stout strips of wood, 36 in. long, by joining their upper ends to a shorter crosspiece. Nail this to the box. Place three paving bricks inside the box, and the polisher will weigh about 16 lb., just the right amount for home use. The polisher is used by rubbing with the grain of the wood.

— RAINCOAT SERVES AS A DUST SHIELD FOR GARMENTS IN CLOSET —

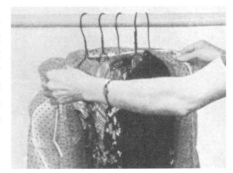

Instead of folding a cellophane or oiled-silk raincoat and storing it away when not needed, use it as a dustcover for garments hung in the closet. It will protect several garments when slipped over them as indicated in the photo.

— POCKETS FOR SPOOLS OF THREAD —

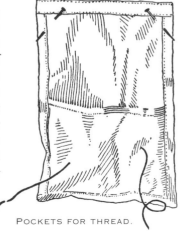

A detachable pocket for holding thread when sewing is shown herewith. The dimensions may be varied to admit any number or size of spools. Each pocket is made to take a certain sized spool, the end of the thread run through the cloth front to obtain the appropriate length for threading a needle. This will keep the thread from becoming tangled and enable it always to be readily drawn out to the required length.

POCKETS FOR THREAD.

— HOMEMADE WORK BASKET —

Secure a cheesebox about 12 in. high and 15 in. or more in diameter. Be careful in selecting this box—be sure to have the cover. Score the wood deeply with a carpenter's gauge, inside and out, 3½ in. from the top of the box. With repeated scoring, the wood will be almost cut through, or in shape to finish the cut with a knife. Now you will have the box in two pieces. The lower part, 8½ in. deep overall, we will call the basket, and the smaller part will be known as the tray.

Remove the band from the cover, and cut the boards to fit in the tray flush with the lower edge, to make the bottom. Fasten with ¾-in. brads The kind of wood used in making these boxes cracks easily and leaves a rough surface that should be well sandpapered.

The four legs are each ¾ in. square and 30½ in. long. The tops should be beveled to keep them from splintering at the edges. Find the circumference of the tray or basket and divide this into four equal parts, using a string or tape measure. Arrange the lap seam on both to come midway between two of the marks. When assembling, make these seams come between the two back legs.

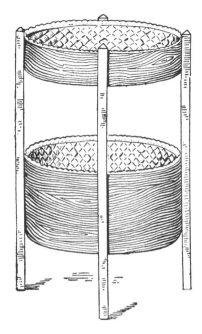

The tray is placed 1¼ in. from the top end and the basket, and 6¾ in. from the bottom end of the legs. Notch the legs at the lower point about 1/8 in. deep and 1¼ in. wide, to receive the band at the lower end of the basket. Fasten with ¾-in. screws, using four to each leg, three of which are in the basket. Insert the screws from the inside of the box into the legs.

Stain the wood before putting in the lining. If all the parts are well sandpapered, the wood will take the stain nicely. Three yards of cretonne will make a very attractive lining. Cut two sheets of cardboard to fit in the bottom of the tray and basket. Cover them with the cretonne, sewing on the backside. Cut four strips for the sides from the width of the goods, 5½ in. wide, and four strips 10 in. wide. Sew them end to end. Then turn down one edge to a depth of 1 in., and gather it at that point. Sew onto the covered cardboards. Fasten them to the sides of the tray and basket with the smallest upholsterers' tacks. The product of your labor will be a very neat and useful piece of furniture.

— FORCING FRUIT BLOSSOMS FOR DECORATIONS —

Twigs trimmed from fruit trees rather late one season had quite large buds on them, and one gardener experimented with them in this way: A large box was filled with wet sand; the twigs were stuck in it, and the box set in the warmest corner of the yard. The buds soon swelled and burst into bloom. The gardener then arranged a smaller box of sand, put the blooming twigs into it, and took it into the house, where the twigs remained fresh for several days.

— CLOSET CLOTHES POLE IS NOTCHED TO KEEP HANGERS APART —

The creasing of garments by having them pressed together on a crowded clothes pole in a closet is avoided by cutting notches, or grooves, 2 in. apart in the top surface of the pole, to take the hanger hooks. For accommodating overcoats and other extra bulky garments, the spacing of the notches should be increased.

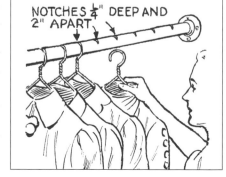

NOTCHES ¼" DEEP AND 2" APART

— Hook Bent from Wire Coat Hanger Eliminates Flush-tank Leak —

If a flush tank leaks persistently even though the parts and working action seem to be in good condition, the trouble may be caused by the float interfering with the seating of the ball valve at the bottom of the tank. When this is the case, it can be corrected by means of an S-hook bent from a wire coat hanger. The hook, which is hung over the side of the tank, is bent so that it stops the float when the latter has dropped far enough to open the inlet. However, the hook keeps the float sufficiently

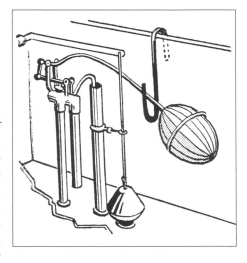

high to prevent interference with the movement of the ball valve.

{ CHAPTER 4 }

MAKE IT;
DON'T BUY IT!

HOME GOODS

— MAKING A REED BASKET —

Inasmuch as there is a great demand for reed furniture, and because good weavers are comparatively few in number, it is wise to learn the process of reed weaving. The weaving operations can be learned much better through the construction of some small article such as a basket or jardiniere cover. The center is the most difficult part of the basket making, and it is best to begin with wood bottoms, because the whole basket can be kept in a much better form due to the stiffness furnished by such a bottom. It is also an approach to the reed furniture that is woven on framework. The objectionable feature of the wood bottoms is the unfinished appearance of the wood edge showing through, but this can be overcome by the use of the roll shown in the illustration.

Though the wood bottoms have been used for this class of work for a number of years, the roll is new and is very popular with those who have seen and used it. The roll can be placed in many ways on different-shaped

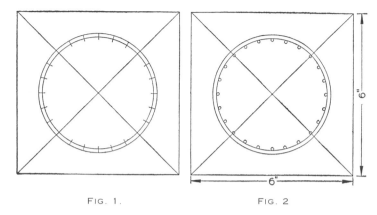

FIG. 1.   FIG. 2

THE BOTTOM IS CUT FROM A PIECE OF WOOD TO GIVE STRENGTH
AND TO AVOID THE MOST DIFFICULT PART OF THE WEAVING.

baskets and other reed pieces. That's why it is best to master this piece of work thoroughly before attempting other or larger pieces. The description is for a basket 5 in. in diameter and 3 in. high, as shown in the illustration. A disk of wood ¼ in. thick and 5 in. in diameter is required. Basswood makes the best bottom, but pine or cedar will do. Cut a board about 6 in. square and draw diagonal lines intersecting at the center on it. Then draw a circle 5 in. in diameter, as shown in *Figure 1;* also another circle, using the same center, 4¾ in. in diameter. Set compass points about ⅝ in. apart, and step off spaces on the inner circle to make 24 points. This will have to be tried out more than

once to get the spaces to come out evenly and have just the right number of points. Holes are bored with an ⅛-in. bit, just inside of the inner circle, back of the places marked by the compass points, as shown in *Figure 2.* Cut the board on the outside circle with a coping saw to make the circle, as in *Figure 3.* Do not saw out

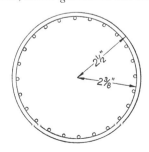

FIG. 3

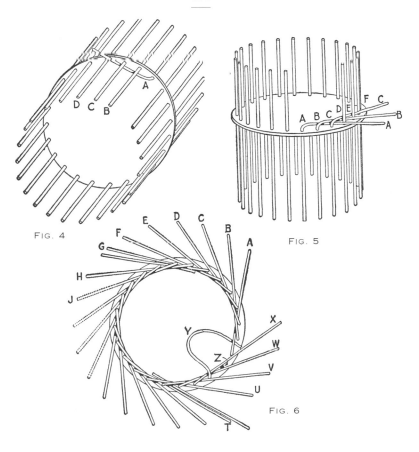

FIG. 4

FIG. 5

FIG. 6

THE REEDS ARE ATTACHED TO THE BOTTOM AND
THEIR LOWER ENDS BENT AS SHOWN.

the circle before boring the holes, as otherwise the disk might split out in places. The reeds placed vertically are called spokes, and the horizontal ones are the weavers. A No. 4 reed is used for the spokes. Do not wet the spokes before putting them through the wood. Allow the ends to project about 5½ in. below the bottom, as shown in *Figure 4*. Place the bottom, with the spokes, in water, and soak them thoroughly, especially the part

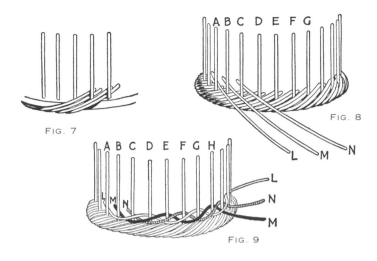

FIG. 7

FIG. 8

FIG. 9

THE LOWER ENDS OF THE SPOKES ARE TURNED TO COVER THE
EDGE OF THE BOTTOM, THEN THE REEDS ARE WOVEN INTO
THE UPRIGHT SPOKES TO THE RIGHT HEIGHT, WHERE THEY
ARE BROKEN DOWN AND WOVEN INTO A TOP BORDER.

below the bottom. About 15 minutes of soaking will be sufficient to
make them pliable enough to bend
over at right angles. It will not injure
the wood bottom to soak it with the
reeds. As shown at *A, Figures 4* and
5, each spoke below the wood bottom is bent down and back of the
two nearest spokes, *B* and *C,* then out
between the third and fourth spokes,
C and *D,* and so on. The last two
spokes, *Y* and *Z, Figure 6,* are forced
under spokes *A* and *B,* respectively.
In this illustration, spoke *Y* is shown

as it is being inserted under spoke *A.*
When this operation is completed,
the bottom will have the appearance
of a fireworks pinwheel.

Continue bending the spokes, in
the same direction, up and across the
thickness of the wood in front of three
other spokes and behind the fourth,
as shown in *Figure 7.* This alone
would not cover the edge of the wood
entirely and, for this reason, other
short spokes must be inserted in front
of each of the first ones before they
are brought up across the edge of the

wood. These supplementary spokes should be about 4 in. long. The manner of inserting these spokes before making the bend is shown at *G* and *T*, *Figure 6*. The double spokes must be pressed down flat when brought up in place, without riding one on the other. If the ends are too long and interfere with the next pair, they can be cut off a little with a flat chisel or a knife. Be careful not to make them too short, or the pieces will not stay in place. If there is still an open space, an extra short spoke can be inserted

to crowd the pieces together and fill up the space.

When the roll is completed, insert three weavers of No. 3 reed that have been soaked about 15 minutes, placing them between spokes *A* and *B*, *B* and *C*, and *C* and *D*, as shown in *Figure 8*. Pass weaver *L* in front of spokes *B* and *C*, then back of *D* and out between *D* and *E*. Weaver *M* is passed in front of *C* and *D*, back of *E* and out in front of *E* and *F*. These operations are clearly shown in *Figure 9*. Weaver *N* is placed in front of

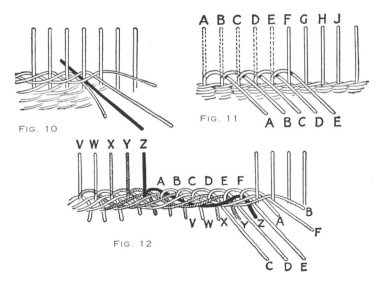

FIG. 10

FIG. 11

FIG. 12

A SIMPLE BREAKDOWN ROLL FORMS THE TOP. AND A METHOD FOR FORMING A ROLL BETWEEN THE FIRST AND SECOND SPOKES REQUIRES THAT ONLY THREE SPOKES ARE TURNED DOWN BEFORE THE THROWING-ACROSS PROCESS BEGINS.

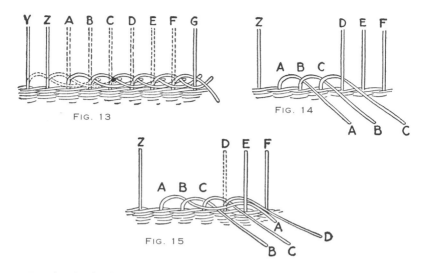

FIG. 13

FIG. 14

FIG. 15

D and *E*, back of *F* and then in front of *G* and *H*. At this point weaver *L* is used again. The weaver farthest behind each time is brought in front of the two spokes nearest to it, then behind the third and out in front of the next two spokes. Do not try to use weavers longer than 8 ft., which is about half the length of a reed. When a weaver is used up, press it back to the side a little, push in a new reed about 1½ in., and continue the weaving. This is clearly shown in *Figure 10*. This weaving is known as the triple weave, which cinches down well and holds tightly. The first round should be carefully worked so as to get the ends of the roll properly pressed down flat in place. Each throw of the weaver should be well pressed down.

The breakdown-tight border is used for the finish at the top. The first operation in making this border is shown in *Figure 11*. Spoke *A* is bent over back of spoke *B* and out between spokes *B* and *C*. Spoke *B* is bent over back of spoke *C* and out between *C* and *D*, and so on, until spoke *E* is turned down. Then take the end of spoke *A*, *Figure 12*, and lay it over *B*, *C*, *D*, and *E*, in front of *F*, back of *G*, and out between *G* and *H*. The end of spoke *F* is then brought down, also between *G* and *H*, but back of the end of *A*. The end of *B* takes a similar leap, passes behind *H* and out between *H* and *J*; then *G* is brought down behind the end of *B*, in the same manner as *F* was brought down in back of *A*. The last four or five spokes are the most difficult to handle, because they must be forced through the first ones to correspond with those already in place. It is best not to pull the ends of *A*, *B*, *C*, and *D* down too tightly at first, keeping in mind that the last ones must be inserted under the first ones. The last standing spokes are represented by the full and shaded lines.

If the roll illustrated in *Figures 11* and *12* is too difficult, a simple break-down can be used, such as is shown in *Figure 13*. To make this finish, spoke *A* is turned back of spoke *B*, in front of spoke *C* and back of spoke *D*, but not out again. Spoke *B* is bent back of *C*, in front of *D*, and back of *E*. The others are turned down the same way. The manner in which the two last spokes are turned down and inserted is shown by the double dotted lines.

The remaining illustrations show the method of forming a roll between the first and second spokes, where only three spokes are turned down before the throwing-across process begins. The first three spokes turned down are shown in *Figure 14,* and the throwing over, in *Figure 15*. The second beginning is shown in *Figure 16*. The finishing of this top is

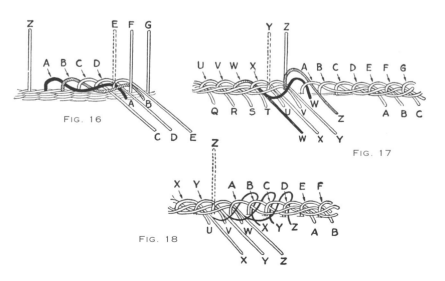

FIG. 16

FIG. 17

FIG. 18

shown in *Figures 17* and *18*. The full, heavy lines represent the final insertions. The reed must be in quite a sharp loop to make the end enter the right place. It is then drawn down and forced in front of the other reed that passes out between the same spokes.

When the basket is dry, the long ends can be cut off close-up with a knife, being careful not to cut a weaver. If there are hairy fibers sticking out, they can be singed off over a gas or other flame that will not smut. If the basket requires bleaching, brush some chloride of lime mixed in a little water over the reeds, and set in the sunlight for a short time. It is better to leave the finish a little dark rather than use too much bleaching, as doing the latter will give an objectionable whitish appearance that looks like a poor job of painting.

In working the reeds, do not leave them in the water longer than necessary, because this will turn them dark. A bleached reed will stand the water much longer than a reed in the natural state. Dampen the reed frequently while weaving it, because the weavers pack down much closer when wet. The dampening process is also required to remedy the drying out caused by whisking the reeds through the air in weaving operations. A great variety of baskets can be made from this form, viz., low, tall, tapering vase forms, bowl shapes, etc., in plain or dark weaves.

— HOW TO MAKE AN EGGBEATER —

There is no reason why any cook should be without this eggbeater, because it can be made quickly in any size. All that is needed is an ordinary can with a tight-fitting cover—a baking-powder can will do. Cut a round piece of wood 3 in. longer than the length of the can. Cut a neat hole in the cover of the can to allow the stick to pass through. At one end of the stick, fasten, by means of a flat-headed tack,

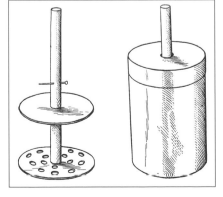

MADE LIKE A CHURN.

a piece of tin, cut round, through which several holes have been punched. Secure another piece of heavier tin of the same size, and make a hole in the center to pass the stick through. Put a small nail 2 in. above the end of the dasher, which allows the second tin to pass up and down in the opposite direction to the dasher. This beater will do the work in less time than the regular kitchen utensil.

— COMBINED LADLE AND STRAINER —

When using a strainer in connection with a ladle, the operation requires both hands. A convenient article where a ladle and strainer are needed is a swinging cup-shaped strainer positioned under the bowl of a ladle, as shown in the illustration. The strainer can be held in place with small bands that fit loosely over the handle and a small tip soldered to the ladle. These will allow the ladle to be turned, leaving the strainer always in position. A large-sized ladle, equipped with a strainer, is just the thing for painters to dip and strain paint, while a small one is of great assistance to the cook for dipping and straining soups, jellies, etc.

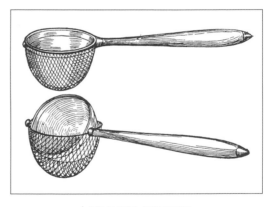

LADLE AND STRAINER.

— BASE FOR ROUND-END BOTTLES —

The many forms of round-bottomed glass bottles used in chemical laboratories require some special kind of support on which they can be safely placed from time to time when the chemist does not, for the moment, need them. These supports should not be made of any hard

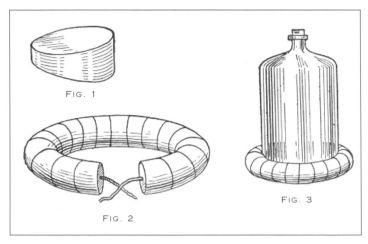

BASE MADE OF CORKS.

material, nor should they be good conductors of heat, as such qualities would result in frequent breakage.

A French magazine suggests making the supports from the large corks of glass jars in which crystal chemicals are usually supplied from dealers. The manner of making them is clearly shown in the sketch. Each cork is cut as in *Figure 1* and placed on a wire ring, as in *Figure 2,* whose ends are twisted together. The last section of cork is cut through from the inner side to the center and thus fitted over the wire covering the twisted ends, which binds them together. The corks in use are shown in *Figure 3.*

— HOW TO MAKE TRANSPARENT PAPER —

Transparent paper of parchment-like appearance and strength, which can be dyed with almost all kinds of aniline dyes and which assumes much more brilliant hues than ordinary colored paper, can be made as follows: Procure a white paper, made of cotton or linen rags, and soak in a saturated solution of camphor in alcohol. When dry, the paper so treated can be cut up into any forms suitable for parts of lampshades, etc.

— How to Make a Candleholder —

A candlestick of very simple construction and design can be made as follows: Secure a piece of brass or copper of No. 23 gauge, of a size sufficient to make the pieces detailed in the accompanying sketch. A riveting hammer and a pair of pliers will be needed,

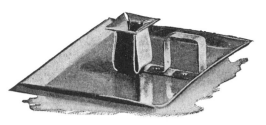

COMPLETED CANDLEHOLDER.

as well as a pair of tin shears and a piece of metal upon which to rivet.

Cut out a piece of metal for the base to a size of 5½ x 5½ in. Trim the sharp corners off slightly. Draw a pencil line all around the margin and ⅝ in. away from the edge. Using the pliers, shape the sides as shown.

Next, lay out the holding cup according to the plan of development shown, and cut out the shape with the shears. Polish both of these pieces, using any common metal polish. Rivet the cup to the base, and then, with the pliers, shape the sides as shown. The manner of making and fastening the handle is clearly illustrated. Use a file to smooth all the cut edges so that they will not injure the hands.

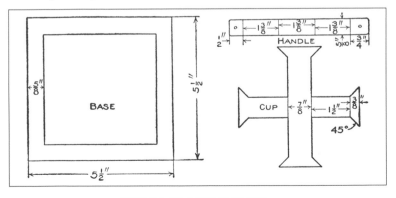

DETAILS OF CANDLEHOLDER.

In riveting, care should be taken to round up the heads of the rivets nicely, as a good mechanic would. Do not be content merely to bend them over. This rounding is easily accomplished by striking around the rivets' outer circumferences, keeping the center high.

A good lacquer should be applied after the parts have been properly cleaned and polished, to keep the metal from tarnishing.

— SPOON REST FOR KETTLES —

A rest for keeping spoons from slipping into kettles can be made from a strip of metal bent as shown in the illustration. The spring of the metal will make it easy to apply to the kettle; the spoon placed in the rest will drain back into the kettle, and the cover can be placed on without removing the spoon.

— RUSTIC WINDOW BOXES —

Instead of using an ordinary green-painted window box, why not make an artistic one in which the color does not clash with the plants contained in it, but rather harmonizes with them.

Such a window box can be made by anyone having simple mechanical ability, and will furnish more opportunities for artistic and original design than many other articles of more complicated construction.

The box proper should be made a little shorter than the length of the window, to allow for the extra space taken up in trimming. It should be nearly equal in width to the sill, as shown in *Figure 1*. If the sill is inclined, as is usually the case, the box will require a greater height in front to make it sit level, as shown in *Figure 2*.

The box should be well nailed or screwed together and should then be painted all over, to make it more durable. A number of ½-in. holes should be drilled in the bottom to allow excess water to run out, and

115

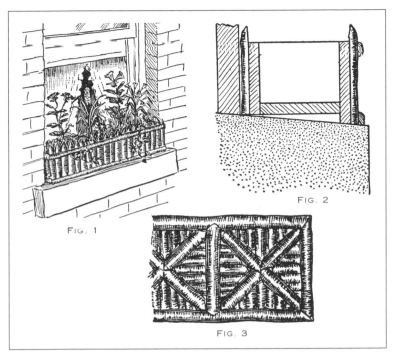

FIG. 2

FIG. 1

FIG. 3

CREATIVE FLOWER BOXES.

thus prevent rotting of the plants and box.

Having completed the bare box, it may be trimmed to suit the fancy of the maker. The design shown in *Figure 1* is very simple and easy to construct, but may be replaced with a panel or other design. One form of panel design is shown in *Figure 3*.

Trimming having a rough surface will be found unsuitable for this work, because it is difficult to

fasten and cannot be split as well as smooth trimming. It should be cut the proper length before being split and should be fastened with brads. The half-round hoops of barrels will be found very useful in trimming, especially for filling-in purposes. By using them, the operation of splitting is avoided. After the box is trimmed, the rustic work should be varnished in order to thoroughly preserve it as well as improve its appearance.

— Paper Shades for Electric-Light Globes —

The appearance of an electric-light globe can be very prettily improved by making a shade of crepe paper of any desired color for each one. Canary-colored crepe produces a soft, mellow effect. Pale blue, yellow, red, and, in fact, all the colors can be used, making a very pleasing variety.

The body of the shade is made of a piece of paper about 5½ in. wide and 3½ ft. long. The width will vary with the length of the globe to be covered, and it is best to have it full, as the edge can be trimmed even with the lower end of the globe afterward.

Another piece of the same color is cut 2½ in. wide and of the same length. This piece makes the ruffle.

The smaller piece is placed on the larger centrally, and both are stitched together with a running stitch, using a needle and cotton thread. A plain running stitch is also made ¼ in. from one edge of the larger strip. The material is gathered along both threads. This operation makes the material shrink in length. Wrap the piece around the globe, pulling the threads taut so that the ends of the paper will just meet. Tie

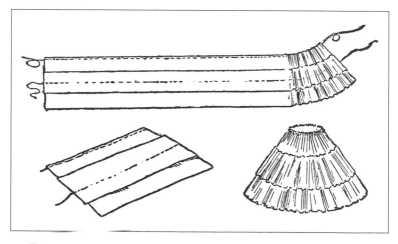

TWO PIECES OF CREPE PAPER STITCHED TOGETHER AND RUFFLED.
TO MAKE A FANCY ELECTRIC-LIGHT SHADE.

the threads, and clip off the extending ends. If the paper extends beyond the end of the globe, trim it off with shears. Ruffle the two edges of the narrow strip and the lower edge of the larger one. This operation is simply stretching the edge of the crepe to cause it to stand out.

— A Broom Holder —

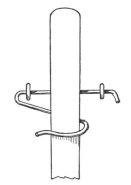

A very simple and effective device for holding a broom when it is not in use is shown in the sketch. It is made of heavy wire and fastened to the wall with two screw eyes, the eyes forming bearings for the wire.

The small turn on the end of the straight part is to hold the hook out far enough from the wall to make it easy to place the broom in the hook. The weight of the broom keeps it in position.

— A Homemade Egg Separator —

To create a device for easily separating egg yolks from whites, secure some small wire and a very large can. Cut the wire into several pieces, and bend them as shown at *A*. Cut the can, bend the side down as shown, and punch holes to receive the upper ends of the wires. Make the holes so that the wires will be about 5/16 in. apart.

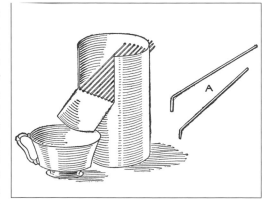

THE CONTENTS OF THE EGGS ARE PLACED ON THE WIRES, WHICH WILL SEPARATE THE YOLKS FROM THE WHITES.

— Small Hook for Hanging a Picture —

After an unsuccessful attempt to hang a small picture with a common pin, a frustrated homeowner devised the following method: After bending about ⅜ in. of the point of an ordinary pin to an angle of about 45 degrees and bending up the other end in the opposite direction to form a hook, he drove the point on a downward slant into the wall. It went in easily and did not mar the plaster.

When making a test, he found that the hook would readily support several pounds of weight.

— How to Make Corner Pieces for a Blotter Pad —

To protect the corners of blotting pads such as will be found on almost every writing desk, proceed as follows:

First, make a design of a size proportionate to the size of the pad. Make a right-angled triangle, as shown in *Figure 1*, on drawing paper. Leave a small margin all around the edge, and then place some decorative form therein. Make allowance for flaps on two sides, as shown, which may later be turned back and folded under, when the metal is worked. It should be noted that the corners of the design are to be clipped slightly. Also note the slight overrun at the top, with the resulting V-shaped indentation.

To make a design similar to the one shown, draw one half of it, then fold along the centerline and rub the back of the paper with a knife handle or some other hard, smooth surface. The other half of the design will be traced on the second side. With metal shears, cut out four pieces of copper or brass of No. 22 gauge. Use carbon paper to trace the shape and decorative design on the metal. Then cut out the outline and file the edges smooth.

Cover the metal over with two coats of primer, allowing each coat time to dry. Paint a final coat of black enamel. The four pieces should be worked at the same time—one for each corner.

It remains to bend the flaps. Place the piece in a vise, as shown in *Figure 2,* and bend the flap sharply, to a right angle. Next, place a piece of metal of a thickness equal to that of the blotter pad at the bend. Use a mallet to bring the flap down parallel to the face of the corner piece, as in *Figure 3.* If the measuring has been done properly, the flaps ought to meet snugly at the corner. If they do not, it may be necessary to bend them back and either remove some metal with the shears or work the metal over farther. All the edges should be left smooth, a metal file and emery paper being used for this purpose.

If a touch of color is desired, it may be had by creating a design with oil colors such as are used for enameling bathtubs. After this has dried, smooth it off with pumice stone and water. To keep the metal from tarnishing, cover it with banana-oil lacquer.

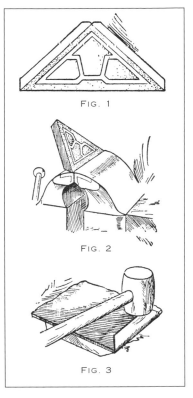

FIG. 1

FIG. 2

FIG. 3

MANNER OF FORMING THE PLATES FOR A BLOTTER PAD.

— HOW TO MAKE A WATCH FOB —

The fixtures for the watch fob shown on page 120 may be made of brass, copper, or silver. Silver is the most desirable but, of course, the most expensive. The buckle is to be purchased. The connection is to be of leather, in a color that harmonizes with the fixtures. The body of the fob may be leather of a suitable color, or silk. Green and brown leathers are the most popular, though almost any color may be obtained.

Make full-sized draw-ings of the outline and design of the fixtures. With carbon paper, trace these on the metal. Pierce the metal of the parts that are to be removed with a small hand drill to make a place for the leather or silk. With a small metal saw, cut out these parts and smooth up the

WATCH FOB.

edges, rounding them slightly so that they will not cut the leather or silk. Next, cut out the outlines with metal shears. File these edges, rounding and smoothing with emery paper.

For coloring silver, brass, or copper, use one of the many aging or special-effects patinas available in craft and hardware stores.

— A Homemade Mailing Tube —

A photograph or manuscript may be sent through the mail unmounted without the danger of being damaged by placing it in a tube made as follows: For an 8 x 10 in. pho-tograph, procure a piece of cardboard 6 x 10 in., plain mounting board preferred, and cut halfway through the card in three places, as shown by the dotted lines in *Figure 1*. Then fold it in a triangular shape, as shown in *Figure 2*. It is easy to make such a tube to fit any photograph or manu-script to be mailed.

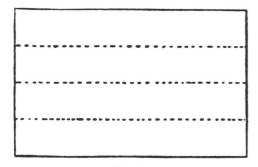

Fig. 1

Fig. 2

THE BENDS IN THE CARDBOARD ARE MADE ON LINES
EQUAL DISTANCES APART, TO FORM A TRIANGLE.

— A POPCORN POPPER —

The accompanying sketch shows the construction of a popcorn popper designed for thoroughly flavoring corn with hot butter or lard and at the same time mixing it with the necessary amount of salt. Procure a metal bucket that just fits the bottom of a frying pan. The stirring device is made of heavy wire, bent as shown, and provided with an empty spool for a handle. A brace is made of tin bent in the shape shown and riveted to the bottom of the bucket.

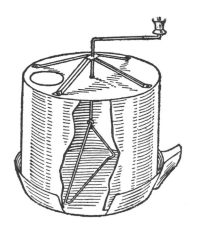

— HOW TO MAKE A BRASS BOOKMARK —

Secure a piece of brass of No. 20 gauge, 2¼ in. wide and 5 in. long. Make a design similar to that shown, the head of which is 2 in. wide, the shaft 1 in. wide below the head, and the total length 4½ in. Make one half of the design, as shown in *Figure 1*, freehand. Then trace the other half in the usual way, after folding along the centerline. Next, trace the design on the metal, using carbon paper, which gives the outline of the design, as seen in *Figure 2*.

Use metal shears to cut out the outline as indicated by the

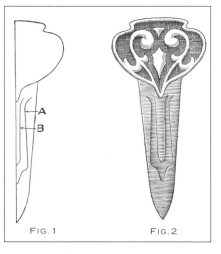

FIG. 1   FIG. 2

THE PATTERN, AND
THE FINISHED BOOKMARK.

drawing. File off any roughness, and form the edge so that it is nicely rounded.

The parts of the design in heavy color may be treated in several ways. A very satisfactory treatment is obtained by enameling.

For coloring olive green, use two parts water to one part permuriate of iron. Apply with a small brush.

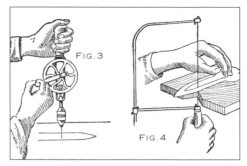

DRILLING AND SAWING THE METAL.

The lines at *A* and *B* will need to be cut, using a small metal saw. Pierce a hole with a small drill, as seen in *Figure 3*, large enough to receive the saw and cut along the lines, as in *Figure 4*. A piece of wood with a V-shaped notch is fastened firmly to the bench. This forms the best place in which to do such sawing. The teeth of the saw should be so placed

that the sawing will be done on the downward stroke. The metal must be held firmly and the saw allowed time to make its cut, being held perpendicular to the work.

After the sawing, smooth the edges of the metal with a small file and emery paper. The metal clip may be bent outward to do this part of the work.

BACK *to* NATURE

— A CAMP LOOM —

The camper who desires to "rough it" as much as possible and to carry only the necessities will find it quite a comfort to construct bedding from grass or moss by weaving it in the manner of making a rag carpet, using heavy twine or small rope as the warp. Two stakes are set at the width

of the bed or mattress to be made, and a cross stick is attached to their tops. Several stakes are set parallel with the cross stick and at a distance to make the length of the mattress. The warp is tied between the tops of the stakes and the cross stick. An equal number of cords are then attached to the cross

LOOM CONSTRUCTED OF STICKS FOR WEAVING GRASS OR MOSS INTO A CAMP MATTRESS.

stick and to another loose cross stick, which is used to move the cords up and down while the grass or moss is placed in for the woof. The ends of the warp are then tied to hold it together. When breaking up camp, the cords can be removed and carried to the next camp.

— A HAND HOE —

A hand hoe especially adapted for weeding or cultivating small plots, particularly onions, can be made of a piece of hardwood, ⅞ in. thick by 1¾ in. wide by 4 ft. long, and a piece of old bucksaw blade. The blade, 18 in. long and 2 in. wide, bent into a loop, is attached with bolts to the handle.

BUCKSAW BLADE ATTACHED TO A HARDWOOD HANDLE.

— A HANDY ICE CHISEL —

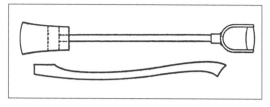

COMBINATION AX AND ICE CHISEL.

Fishing through the ice is great sport, but cutting the first holes preparatory to setting the lines is not always an easy task. The ice chisel described here will be very handy and may be made at very slight expense.

Drill a 9/16-in. hole in the top of an old ax head, and then tap the hole for a 3/8-in. gas pipe, about 18 in. long. Thread the other end of the pipe and screw on an old snow-shovel handle. When ready for use, screw the two pieces together and you have your chisel complete.

A short ax handle may be included in the outfit. When the holes are finished and your lines set, unscrew the pipe from the head of the ax, put in the handle, and your ax is ready to cut the wood to keep your fire going.

— A HOMEMADE GARDEN WEEDER —

It is possible to make an efficient weeder for keeping the home garden free from weeds, using only a few pieces of flat iron, such as is used in old buggy tires, and a wheel that can be taken from an old wheelbarrow or truck.

The device is constructed as indicated in

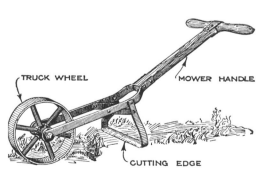

A HOMEMADE GARDEN WEEDER ALSO SERVES AS A CULTIVATOR

the drawing. A blade is mounted parallel to the ground and pushed along just underneath the surface, cutting the roots of weeds and other plants outside the rows. Not only will this instrument keep down the weeds, but it also acts as a cultivator by breaking up the hard crust between the rows and conserving the moisture for useful vegetation.

— HOMEMADE GARDEN CULTIVATOR —

A member of an Ohio garden club built the hand cultivator shown, at a total cost of less than a box of cereal. The builder obtained the same results from this model that one would expect from the manufactured and higher-priced hand cultivators. Practically the only expense was the cost of having the cultivator shovels forged by a local metalworker or blacksmith. The adjustable wooden frame that holds the cultivator shovels is arranged so that the implement can be set for shallow, medium, or deep cultivation. The handles are 5½ ft. long, and 22 in. apart at the outer end. The wheel may be one taken from an old baby carriage or, better, from an old wheelbarrow.

FOR USE ON AN ALLOTMENT IN A GARDEN CLUB, ONE OF THE MEMBERS BUILT THIS EFFICIENT CULTIVATOR.

It should be lined up exactly midway between the handles.

— SELF-LIGHTING ARC SEARCHLIGHT —

A practical and easily constructed self-lighting arc searchlight can be made in the following manner: Procure a large can, about 6 in. in diameter. Cut three holes in its side, about 2 in. from the back end, and

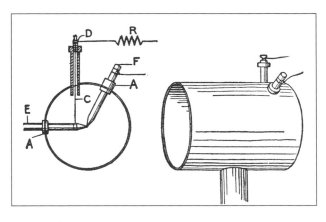

ARC IN A LARGE CAN, FOR A SEARCHLIGHT.

in the positions shown in the sketch. Two of the holes are cut large enough to hold a short section of a garden hose tightly, as shown at *AA*. A piece of porcelain tube, *B*, is fitted tightly into the third hole and used for insulation. The hose insulation *A* should hold the carbon *F* rigidly, while the carbon *E* should rest loosely in its insulation.

The inner end of carbon *E* is supported by a piece of No. 25 German-silver wire, *C*, which is about 6 in. long. This wire runs through the porcelain tube to the binding post *D*. The binding post is fastened to a wood plug in the end of the tube. Tube *B* is adjusted so that the end of carbon *E* is pressing against carbon *F*. The electric wires are connected to carbon *F* and binding post *D*. There should be some resistance, *R*, in the line. The current, in passing through the lamp, heats the strip of German silver wire. This causes the wire to expand. This expansion lowers the end of carbon *E*, separating the points of the two carbons and thus providing a space between them for the formation of an arc. When the current is turned off, the German-silver wire contracts and draws the two carbon ends together, ready for lighting again. The feed can be adjusted by sliding carbon *F* through its insulation. Resistance for the arc may be created by running the current through a water rheostat or through 15 ft. of No. 25 gauge German-silver wire.

— PRACTICAL BRACKET FOR GARDEN HOSE —

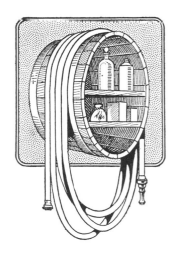

Care in the storage of a garden hose will pay the owner in the longer life of it, and the homemade bracket shown in the sketch suggests a convenient method of caring for the hose. A portion of a barrel was sawed off at one of the hoops, and after reinforcing it by nailing the hoops and inserting shelves, it was nailed to the wall. The hose may be coiled over it to be easily carried to the lawn or garden for use. The shelves provide space for an oilcan for the lawn mower and other accessories.

FURNITURE

— AN ADJUSTABLE BOOK HOLDER —

A very satisfactory adjustable holder for books or letters can be constructed of ordinary materials. base. A good-sized holder is 19 in. long, 6 in. wide, and made of material ¾ in. thick.

A board is used for the base, and two pieces, C, cut from the grooved edges of flooring boards, are fastened on top, as shown. A permanent end, A, is fastened to one end of the

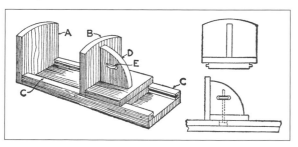

THE HOLDER MAY BE USED FOR BOOKS OR FOR LETTERS AND PAPERS, AS A FILE.

The movable slide *B* has two pieces attached to its underside, which are cut from the tongued edges of flooring boards. The piece *D* answers the double purpose of a handle and brace. A lock, *E*, is made of a bolt having a long thread and a square head. A hole is bored from the underside through the brace, and a portion of the wood is cut out to admit the nut. A square place is cut out to admit the square bolt head in the bottom pieces. To lock the slide, simply screw the nut upward so that it will push the bolt head against the base.

— BOOKRACK —

Everyone enjoys a handy place to display favorite books and keep their reading matter in order. The material necessary for the illustrated bookrack is as follows:

-two endpieces, ⅝ in. x 5¼ in. x 6 in.
-one shelf, ⅝ in. x 5¼ in. x 14½ in.

The shelf is cut rectangular, 5¼ in. wide by 14¼ in. long. Its two ends should then be provided with tenons ⅜ in. thick by 5¼ in. wide, and extending out ¼ in.

The endpieces, after being cut to the given dimensions, are marked off and cut out for mortises to fit the shelf tenons.

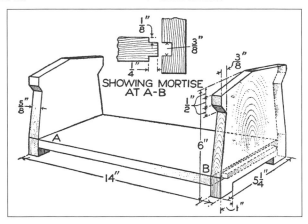

A BOOKRACK THAT CAN BE MADE IN ANY WOOD
TO MATCH OTHER FURNITURE.

The parts are glued into place and clamped with hand screws until the glue has set. Any of the good Mission stains, properly applied, will give an attractive finished appearance to the bookrack.

— FLOWERPOT STAND —

A very useful stand for flowerpots can be made of a piece of board supported by four clothes hooks. The top may be of any size suitable for the flowerpot. The hooks, which serve as legs, are fastened to the underside of the board in the same manner as they are fastened to a wall.

— POT-COVER CLOSET —

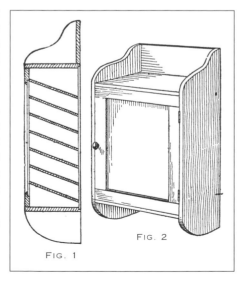

Constructing a closet for pot covers is easy to do. The sides of the closet are cut as shown in *Figure 1*, and shelves are nailed between them at a slight angle.

No dimensions are given, because the space and the sizes of the covers are not always the same. The back is covered with thin boards placed vertically. The front can be covered with a curtain or a paneled door, as shown in *Figure 2*.

FIG. 1

FIG. 2

CLOSET FOR HOLDING POT COVERS.

— HOMEMADE SHOE RACK —

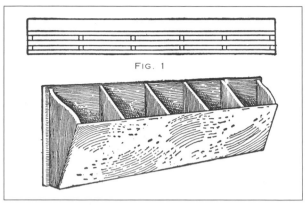

FIG. 1

The above sketch explains how a boy can make his own shoe rack, which can be placed on the wall in the clothes closet. *Figure 1* shows the construction of the bottom to permit the dirt to fall through. Two boards, 9 in. wide and about 3 ft. long, with six partitions between, as shown in *Figure 2*, will make pockets about 6 in. long. The width of the pockets at the bottom is 2 in., and at the top, 5 in.

— HOW TO MAKE A CUP-AND-SAUCER RACK —

This rack is made of any suitable kind of wood. The sides, *A*, are cut just alike, or from one pattern. The shelves are made in various widths, to fit the sides at the places where they are wanted. The number of shelves can be varied and cut to suit the size of the dishes. Cup hooks

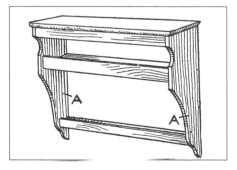

are placed on the top and bottom shelves. The rack is then hung on the wall in the same manner as a picture from the molding.

—A Neat and Economical Baby Crib Made from a Clothes Basket —

A clothes basket on a simple strong wooden frame mounted on castors makes a cradle that is as convenient and sanitary as many that are sold for five times its cost. It is light enough to roll out on the porch without difficulty and may be padded and fitted with pillows until the most exacting mother is satisfied. The basket and frame should be painted, preferably some light color. The whole cost, including pads or pillows, is extremely modest.

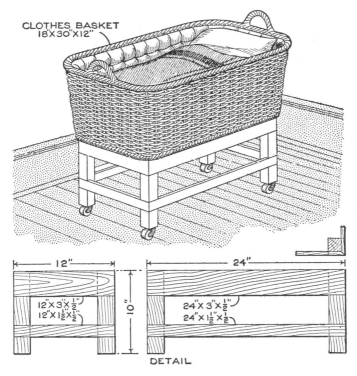

CLOTHES BASKET
18"X30"X12"

12"

24"

10"

12"X 3"X ½"
12"X 1½"X ½"

24"X 3"X ½"
24"X 1½"X ½"

DETAIL

A FEW STICKS OF WOOD AND A CLOTHES BASKET MAKE
A CONVENIENT CRADLE FOR THE BABY.

— How to Make a Porch-swing Chair —

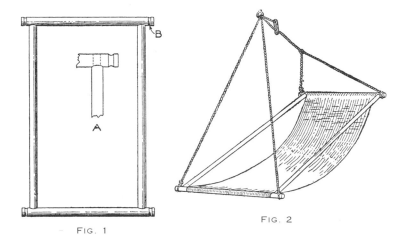

Fig. 1

Fig. 2

The materials needed for making this porch-swing chair are two pieces of roundwood 2½ in. in diameter and 20 in. long, and two pieces 1¼ in. in diameter and 40 in. long. The longer pieces can be made square, but for appearance it is best to have them round, or square with the corners rounded. A piece of canvas or other stout cloth, 16 in. wide and 50 in. long, is used for the seat. The two short pieces of wood are used for the ends of the chair, and two 1-in. holes are bored in each end of them 1½ in. from the ends. Between the holes and the ends, grooves are cut around them to make a place to fasten ropes, as shown at B, Figure 1.

The two longer pieces are used for the sides, and a tenon is cut on each end of them to fit in the 1-in. holes bored in the endpieces, as shown at A, Figure 1. The canvas is now tacked on the endpieces, and the pieces given one turn before mortising together.

The chair is now hung up to the porch ceiling, with ropes attached to a large screw eye or hook. The end of the chair to be used for the lower part is held about 16 in. from the floor, with ropes directed from the grooves in the endpieces to the hook. The upper end is supported by a rope in the form of a loop or bail, as shown in Figure 2. The middle of the loop or bail should be about

15 in. from the endpiece of the chair. Another rope is attached to the loop, through the hook, and to a slide, as shown. This will allow for adjustments to make the device into a chair or a hammock.

— A HOMEMADE CLOTHES RACK —

A clothes-drying rack with many good features can be made as shown in the illustration. When the rack is closed, it will fit into a very small space. One or more wings can be used at a time, as the occasion or space permits, and the rack will not tip over. The rack can be made of any hardwood, and the material list is as follows:

- one center post 1¼ in. square x 62 in.
- four braces 1¼ in. square x 12 in.
- four vertical pieces ¼ x 1 x 65 in.

- sixteen horizontal bars 1 x 1¼ x 24 in.

Attach the four braces for the feet with finishing nails, after applying a good coat of glue.

The horizontal bars are fastened to the vertical pieces with rivets, using washers on both sides. The holes are bored a little large so as to make a slightly loose joint. The other ends of the bars are fastened to the center post with roundhead screws. They are fastened, as shown, so the rack can be folded up.

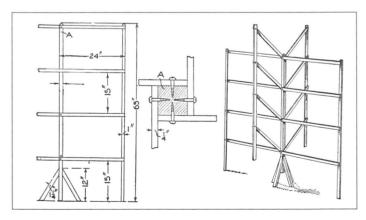

FOLDING CLOTHES RACK.

— How to Make a Fire Screen —

A screen that will not interfere with the radiation of heat from a fire but will keep skirts and children safe can be made at little expense out of some strap iron. The screen that is shown in *Figure 1* stands 20 in. high from the base to the top crosspiece. It is made of ¾ x ¼ in. and ½ x ¼ in. iron. The top and bottom pieces, marked *A, Figure 1*, are ¾ x ¼ in. and are 30 in. long, bent at an angle to fit the fireplace 7 in.

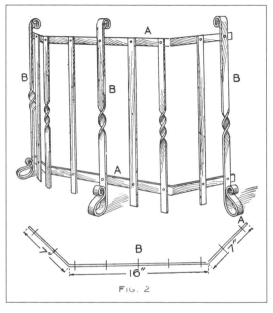

FIG. 2

FIRE SCREEN MADE OF STRAP IRON.

from each end, as shown in *Figure 2*. The three legs marked *B, Figure 1*, are of the same size iron; each leg will take 34 in. of material. In shaping the feet of these three pieces, give them a slight tendency to lean toward the fire or inside of screen. In the two crossbars, 1 in. from each end, *A* in *Figure 2*, mark for a hole. Three inches from that point, mark the next hole. Mark the center of the bar, *B*, 15 in. from each end for a hole;

3½ in. on each side of *B*, mark again; and 3½ in. beyond each of these two, mark again.

Mark the legs 2¾ in. from the bottom and 2 in. from the top. After making rivet holes, rivet them to crossbars *A, Figure 1*.

Cut six pieces 17½ in. long, and punch holes to fit. Rivet onto the remaining holes in crossbars *A, Figure 1*. Clean the screen up and give it a coat of black enamel.

Fun *and* Entertainment

— Child's Homemade Swing Seat —

A very useful swinging seat for children can be made from a box or packing case. Procure a box of the right size, and saw it out in the shape shown in the illustration. The apron or board in front slides on the two front ropes. The board can be raised to place the child in the box and to remove him. The ropes are fastened to the box by tying knots in their ends and driving staples over them. Always check the ropes for fraying before every use.

— A Homemade Yankee Bobsled —

A good coasting sled, sometimes called a Yankee bob, can be made from two hardwood barrel staves, two pieces of 2 x 6 in. pine, a piece of hardwood for the rudder, and a few pieces of board. The 2 x 6 in. pieces should be a little longer than one-third the length of the staves, and each piece cut tapering from the widest part, 6 in., down to 2 in., and then fastened to the staves with large wood screws, as shown in *Figure 1*. Boards 1 in. thick are nailed on top of the pieces for a seat and to hold the runners together.

The boards should be of such a length as to make the runners about 18 in. apart.

A 2-in. shaft of wood, *Figure 2*, is turned down to 1 in. on the ends and put through holes that must be bored in the front ends of the 2 x 6 in. pieces, *Figure 3*. A small pin is put through each end of the shaft to keep it in place. The rudder is a 1½ in. hardwood piece that should be tapered to ½ in. at the bottom and shod with a thin piece of iron. A ½-in. hole is bored through the center of the shaft, and a lag screw

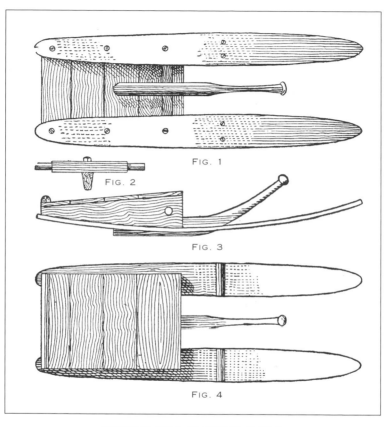

FIG. 1

FIG. 2

FIG. 3

FIG. 4

RUNNERS MADE OF BARREL STAVES.

put through and turned in the rudder piece, making it so that the rudder will turn right and left and up and down. Two cleats are nailed to the upper sides of the runners and in the middle lengthways as shown in *Figure 4* for the person's heels to rest against.

Any child can guide this bob. All he has to do is to guide the rudder right and left to go in the direction he wants. To stop, he pulls up on the handle, and the heel of the rudder will dig into the snow, causing too much friction for the sled to go any farther.

— TELESCOPE STAND AND HOLDER —

With the ordinary small telescope it is very difficult to keep the line of sight fixed upon any particular object. To remedy the situation, one amateur astronomer constructed the device illustrated here. A circular piece of wood, *B*, 6 in. in diameter, is fastened to a common camera tripod, *A*, with a setscrew, *S*. Corner irons, *C*, are screwed to the circular piece. These corner irons are also screwed to and supported in a vertical position by the wood standard *D*, which is 4 in. wide and of any desired height. To this standard is secured the wood shield-shaped piece, *E*, by the screw *G*, upon which it turns. A semicircular slit is cut in the piece *G*, through which passes the setscrew *S*. The telescope is secured to the piece *G* by means of the pipe straps, *F*. Rubber bands are put around the telescope to prevent rubbing at the places where the straps enclose it.

The wood pieces are made of mahogany, well rubbed with linseed

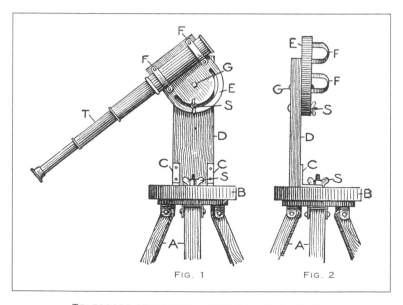

FIG. 1   FIG. 2

TELESCOPE STAND MADE FROM A CAMERA TRIPOD.

oil to give them an attractive finish. The corner irons and setscrews, or bolts with thumb nuts, can be purchased at any hardware store. The pipe straps of different sizes can be obtained from a plumbing supply or home center. With this device, either a vertical or a horizontal motion may be secured. After bringing the desired object into the line of sight, the setscrews will hold the telescope in position. Anyone owning a tripod can construct this device in three or four hours' time, at a trifling cost. *Figure 1*

shows the side view of the holder and stand, and *Figure 2,* the front view.

It may be of interest to those owning telescopes without solar eyepieces to know that such an eyepiece can be obtained very cheaply by purchasing a pair of colored eyeglasses with very dark lenses and metal rims. Break off the frame, leaving the metal rims and nibs at each end. Place these over the eyepiece of the telescope, and secure in place with rubber bands looped over the nibs and around the barrel of the instrument.

— HOW TO MAKE A MINNOW TRAP —

Glass minnow traps that will give as good service as those purchased at the tackle store can be made without difficulty. If a trap should be smashed as it is banged carelessly against the side of the boat, a half hour's time will turn out a new one just as good, eliminating the need to spend several dollars to replace it.

A trap of this kind can be made from an ordinary fruit jar such as is used in putting up preserves, either of 1- or 2-qt. capacity. A 1-qt. jar gives good results, but if the bait to be caught is of fairly large size, the 2-qt. size may be used. Because the jars have the same style top, they can

be used interchangeably with one mouthpiece.

The mouthpiece is made of a round-neck bottle of colorless, thin glass. If the neck of the bottle is cut at the right point, it makes a glass funnel that will just fit into the fruit jar. The funnel forms the mouth of the trap. Put the neck of the bottle into the fruit jar, and mark the glass with a file where the bottle and jar meet. Now use a glass cutter to score a deep cut around the bottle on the mark. Once you're sure the score is well established, tap the line with the breaker on the end of the cutter.

Bind some copper wire around the neck of the jar so that three ends will project ½ in. or more. These are bent down over the funnel when put into the jar, forming clamps to hold it in place. The copper wire can be bent many times in emptying or baiting the trap, without breaking.

Two copper wire bands are tied tightly around the jar about 3 in. apart. They should be twisted tightly with a pair of pliers, and the ends joined, forming a ring for attaching a cord.

For catching "kellies" or "killies" (killifish), bait the trap with crushed clams or saltwater mussels. For fresh-water shiners, use mincemeat or bread crumbs, and do not spill any bait outside the trap. Leave the trap down ten to fifteen minutes. When resetting it after emptying, put back one or two of the victims, as the others enter more readily if they see some of their companions ahead of them.

— HOMEMADE POTTERY KILN —

A small kiln for baking clay figures may be built at a very small cost. The following shows the general plan of such a kiln, which has stood the test of 200 firings and which is good for any work requiring less than 1,400°C.

Procure an iron pail about 1 ft. high by 1 ft. across, with a cover. Any old pail that is thick enough will do. In the bottom of this, cut a 2-in. round hole, and close

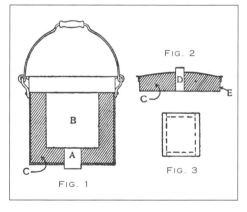

HOMEMADE POTTERY KILN.

it with a cork or wood plug, *A, Figure 1*. This plug shall project at least 2 in. inside the pail. Make a cylindrical core of wood, *B, Figure 1*, 8 in. long and 8 in. wide. Make a mixture of clay, 60 percent; sand, 15 percent; and

graphite, 25 percent, kneading thoroughly in water to a good molding consistency. Line the pail bottom and sides with heavy paper, and cover the core with it. Now pack the bottom of the pail thoroughly with a 2-in. layer of the clay mixture, and set the paper-wrapped core on it, carefully centering it. The 2-in. space between the core and the sides of the pail, all around, is to be filled with clay, *C*, as is shown in the sketch. Use a little at a time, and pack it very tight. In like manner, make the cover of the kiln, cutting the hole a little smaller, about 1 in. At the edge or rim of the cover, encircle a 2-in. strip of sheet iron, *E*, *Figure 2*, to hold the clay mixture, *C*. Set aside for a few days until well dried.

While these items are drying, make a muffle if there is to be any glazing done. This is a clay cylinder, as seen in *Figure 3*, with a false top and bottom, in which the pottery to be glazed is protected from any smoke or dust. It is placed inside the kiln, setting on any convenient blocks that will place it midway. The walls of the muffle should be about ½ in. thick, and the dimensions should allow at least 1 in. of space all around for the passage of heat between it and the walls of the kiln. By the time the clay of the kiln is well dried, it will be found that it has all shrunk away from the iron about ⅜ in. After removing all the paper, pack this space—top, bottom, and sides—with moist-ground fireproof-lining material (available at craft-supply stores). If the cover of the pail

has no rim, it may be fastened to the fireproof material and clay lining by punching a few holes, passing wire nails through, and clinching them. Fit all the parts together snugly, take out the plugs in the top and bottom, and your kiln is ready for business. The handle of the pail will be convenient for moving it about, and it can be set on three bricks or some more elaborate support, as dictated by fancy and expense.

The temperature required for baking earthenware is 1,250° to 1,310°C; hotel china, 1,330°C; hard porcelain, 1,390° to 1,410°C. These temperatures cannot be obtained in the above kiln by means of the ordinary Bunsen burner. If will be necessary either to buy the largest size Bunsen or make one yourself, if you have the materials. If you can get a cone that can be screwed into an inch pipe, file the opening of the cone to $1/16$ in. in diameter, and jacket the whole with a 2½ in. pipe. The flame end of this burner tube should be about 4½ in. above the cone opening and should be covered with gauze to prevent flames from snapping back. When lighted, the point of the blue flame, which is the hottest part, should be just in the hole in the bottom of the kiln. Such a burner will be cheaply made and will furnish a kiln temperature of 1,400°C, but it will burn a great deal of gas.

A plumber's torch of medium size will cost more in the beginning but will be cheaper in operation. Whatever burner is used, the firing should be gradual, and with especial caution the first time. By experiment you will find that a higher temperature is obtained by placing a 1-in. pipe 2 ft. long over the lid hole as a chimney. It would be still more effective to get another iron pail, 2 in. wider than the kiln, and get a downdraft by inverting it over the kiln at whatever height proves most suitable.

— How to Build a Toboggan Sled —

A "WINNER" TOBOGGAN SLED.

The first goal of a sled builder should be to build a "winner" both in speed and appearance. The following instructions for building a sled are designed to produce these results.

The completed sled should be 15 ft., 2 in. long by 22 in. wide, with the cushion about 15 in. above the ground. Select a pine board for the baseboard 15 ft. long, 11 in. wide, and 2 in. thick, and plane it on all edges. Fit up the baseboard with ten oak footrests 22 in. long, 3 in. wide, and ¾ in. thick. Fasten them on the underside of the baseboard at right angles to its length and 16 in. apart, beginning at the rear. At the front, 24 to 26 in. will be left without crossbars, for fitting on the auto front. On the upper side of the crossbars, at their ends on each side, screw

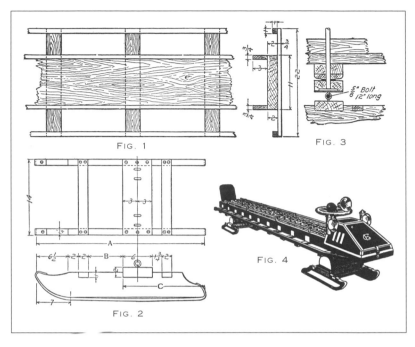

FIG. 1

FIG. 3

FIG. 2

FIG. 4

a piece of oak 1 in. square by 14 ft. long. On the upper side of the baseboard, at its edge on each side, screw an oak strip 3 in. wide by ¾ in. thick and the length of the sled from the back to the auto front. These are to keep the cushion from falling out. See *Figure 1*. For the back of the sled, use the upper part of a child's high chair, taking out the spindles and resetting them in the rear end of the baseboard. Cover up the outside of the spindles with a piece of galvanized iron.

The construction of the runners is shown in *Figures 2* and *3*. The stock required for them is oak, two pieces 30 x 5 x 1¼ in., two pieces 34 x 5 x 1¼ in., two pieces 14 x 6 x 2 in., and four pieces 14 x 2 x 1 in. They should be put together with large screws about 3 in. long. Use no nails, because they are not substantial enough. In proportioning them, the points *A*, *B*, and *C*, *Figure 2*, are important For the front runners, these measurements are as follows: *A*, 30 in.; *B*, 4 in.; *C*, 15½ in. For the rear runners, they are as follows: *A*, 34 in.; *B*, 7 in.; *C*, 16½ in. The screw eyes indicated must be placed in a straight line, and the holes for them carefully centered. A variation of ¹/₁₆ in. one way or another would cause a great deal of trouble. The steel runners are ⅜-in. cold-rolled steel, flattened at the ends for screw holes. Use no screws on the running surface, however, as they "snatch" the ice.

The mechanism of the front steering gear is shown at *Figure 3*. A ¾-in. steel rod makes a good steering rod. Flatten the steering rod at one end, and sink it into the wood. Hold it in place by means of an iron plate drilled to receive the rod and screwed to block *X*. An iron washer, *Z*, is used to reduce friction. Bevel block *K* gives a rocking motion. Equip block *X* with screw eyes, making them clear those in the front runner, and bolt through. For the rear runner, put a block with screw eyes on the baseboard, and run a bolt through.

Construct the auto front, seen in *Figure 4*, of ¾-in. oak boards. The illustration shows how to shape it. Bevel it toward all sides, and keep the edges sharp, because sharp edges are best suited for the brass trimmings that are to be added. When the auto front is in place, enamel the sled either a dark maroon or a creamy white. First sandpaper all the wood, then apply a coat of thin enamel. Let stand for three days and apply another coat. Three coats of enamel and one of thin varnish will make a fine-looking sled. For the brass trimmings use No. 27 B&S sheet brass 1 in. wide on all the front edges, and pieces 3 in. square on the crossbars, to rest the feet against. On the door of the auto front put the monogram of the owner or owners of the sled, cutting it out of sheet brass.

Procure an old brass-plated freight-car "brake" wheel for the steering wheel. Fasten a horn, such as is used on automobiles, to the wheel.

Make the cushion of leather, and stuff it with horse hair. The best way is to get some strong, cheap material, such as burlap, sew up one end, and shape in the form of an oblong bag. Stuff this as tightly as possible with horse hair. Then get some upholstery buttons, fasten a cord through the loop, bring the cord through to the underside of the cushion, and fasten the button by slipping a nail through the knot. Then put a leather covering over the burlap, sewing it to the burlap on the underside. Make the cushion for the back in the same way. On top of the cushion supports, run a brass tube to serve the double purpose of holding the cushion down and affording something to hold on to.

If desired, bicycle lamps may be fastened to the front end to improve the appearance. It is wise to have a light of some kind at the back, to avoid the danger of rear-end collisions.

The door of the auto front should be hinged and provided with a lock so that skates, parcels, overshoes, lunch, etc. may be stowed within. A silk pennant with a monogram adds to the appearance.

If desired, a brake may be added to the sled. This can be a wrought-iron lever 1½ x ½ x 30 in. long, so pivoted that moving the handle will cause the end to scrape the ice. This toboggan sled can be made without the lamps and horn at a minimal cost, or with these for slightly more. The pleasure derived from the sled well repays the builder. If the expense is greater than one can afford, a number of boys may share in the sled's ownership.

— DUMBBELLS MADE OF CEMENT —

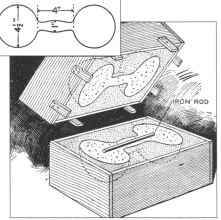

Dumbbells of any weight and size may be made with little trouble from ordinary cement. Two mold boxes are made and filled with moist sand, into which the pattern is pressed. After removing the pattern, the mold is thoroughly greased with heavy oil or light grease to prevent the sand from sticking to the cement. The mold is then filled with cement mortar. Before the cement has completely hardened, a small iron rod is placed on the lower mold as reinforcement for the handle. The molds are then placed together until the cement has completely hardened.

A dumbbell made to the dimensions given will weigh approximately 10 lb. Heavier or lighter bells may be made by embedding suitably sized pieces of wood or metal in the ends.

— MAKING SKIS AND SKI-TOBOGGANS —

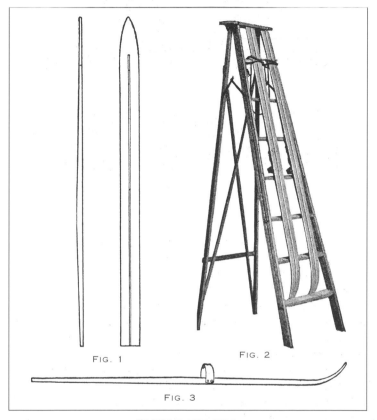

FIG. 1

FIG. 2

FIG. 3

FORMING THE SKIS.

During the winter months, everyone is thinking of skating, coasting, or ski running and jumping. Those too timid to run down a hill standing upright on skis must take their pleasure in coasting or skating.

Ordinary skis can be made into a coasting ski-toboggan by joining two pairs together with bars, without injury to their use for running and jumping.

In making a pair of skis, select two strips of Norway pine, free from

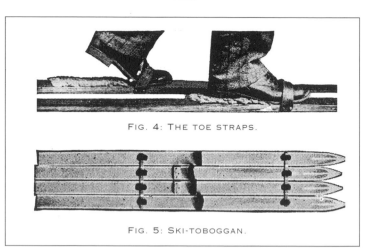

FIG. 4: THE TOE STRAPS.

FIG. 5: SKI-TOBOGGAN.

knots, 1 in. thick by 4 in. wide by 7 or 8 ft. long. Try to procure as fine and straight a grain as possible. The pieces are dressed thin at both ends, leaving about 1 ft. in the center the full thickness of 1 in., and gradually thinning to a scant ½ in. at the ends. One end of each piece is tapered to a point beginning 12 in. from the end. A groove is cut on the underside about ¼ in. wide and ⅛ in. deep and running almost the full length of the ski. This will make it track straight and tends to prevent sideslipping. The shape of each piece for a ski, as it appears before bending, is shown in *Figure 1*.

The pointed end of each piece is placed in boiling water for at least an hour, after which the pieces are ready for bending. The bend is made on an ordinary stepladder. The pointed ends are stuck under the back of one step, and the other end securely tied to the ladder, as shown in *Figure 2*. They should remain tied to the ladder 48 hours, in moderate temperatures, after which they will hold their shape permanently.

The two straps, *Figure 3*, are nailed on a little forward of the center of gravity so that when the foot is lifted the front of the ski will be raised. Tack on a piece of sheepskin or deer hide where the foot rests, *Figure 5*. The best finish for skis is boiled linseed oil. After two or three applications, the underside will take on a polish resembling glass from the contact with the snow. The ski-toboggan is made by placing two pairs of skis together side by side, as shown in *Figure 4*, and fastening them with two bars across the top. The bars are held with V-shaped metal clips, as shown in *Figure 5*.

— BOOMERANGS AND HOW TO MAKE THEM —

A boomerang is a weapon invented and used by native Australians. The boomerang is a curved stick of hardwood, *Figure 1*, typically about 5/16 in. thick by 2½ in. wide by 2 ft. long. It is flat on one side, with the ends and the other side rounding. One end of the stick is grasped in one hand, with the convex edge forward and the flat side up, and thrown upward. After going some distance and ascending slowly to a great height

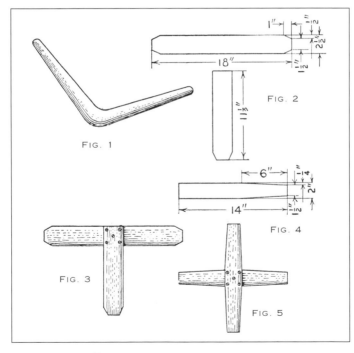

DETAILS OF THREE BOOMERANGS.

in the air with a quick rotary motion, it suddenly returns in an elliptical orbit to a spot near the starting point. If thrown down on the ground, the boomerang rebounds in a straight line, pursuing a ricochet motion until the object at which it was thrown is struck.

Two other types of boomerangs are illustrated here, and they can be made as described. The materials necessary for the T-shaped boomerang are as follows: one piece of hard maple 5/16 in. thick, 2½ in. wide, and 3 ft. long and five ½-in. flat-headed screws. Cut the piece of hard maple into two pieces, one 11½ in. and the other 18 in. long. The corners are cut from these pieces, as shown in *Figure 2*, taking care to cut exactly the same amount from each corner. Bevel both sides of the pieces, making the edges very thin so that they will cut the air better. Find the exact center of the long piece. Make a line 1¼ in. on each side of the center, and fasten the short length between the

lines with the screws, as shown in *Figure 3*. The short piece should be fastened perfectly square and at right angles to the long one.

The materials necessary for the cross-shaped boomerang are as follows: one piece of hard maple 5/16 in. thick, 2 in. wide, and 30 in. long and five ½-in. flat-headed screws. Cut the maple into two 14-in. pieces, and plane the edges of these pieces so that the ends will be 1½ in. wide, as shown in *Figure 4*. Bevel these pieces the same as the ones for the T-shaped boomerang. The two pieces are fastened together as shown in *Figure 5*. All of the boomerangs, when completed, should be given several coats of linseed oil and thoroughly dried. This will keep the wood from absorbing water and becoming heavy. The last two boomerangs are thrown in a similar way to the first one, except that one of the pieces is grasped in the hand and the throw given with a quick underhand motion. A little practice is all that is necessary for one to become skillful in throwing them.

— HOMEMADE SNOWSHOES —

To craft your own snowshoes, secure four light barrel staves and sandpaper the outside smooth. Take two old shoes that are extra large and cut off the tops and heels so as to

leave only the toe covering fastened to the sole. Purchase two long book straps, cut them in two in the middle, and fasten the ends on the toe covering, as shown in *Figure 1*. The straps

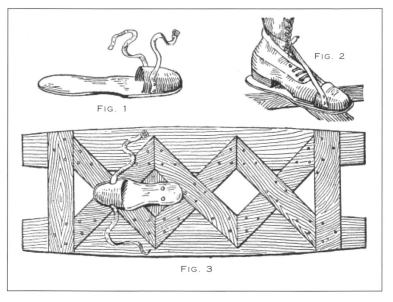

FIG. 1

FIG. 2

FIG. 3

SNOWSHOES MADE FROM BARREL STAVES.

are used to attach the snowshoe to the regular shoe. When buckling up the straps, be sure to leave them loose enough for the foot to work freely, as *Figure 2* illustrates. Fasten the barrel staves in pairs, leaving a space of 4 in. between them, as shown in *Figure 3*, with thin strips of wood. Nail the old shoe soles to crosspieces placed one-third of the way from one end.

— MORE BOOMERANGS —

When the ice is too thin for skating and the snow is not right for skis, about the only thing to do is to stay in the house. A boomerang club will help to fill these in-between times, and also furnishes good exercise for the muscles of the arm. A boomerang can be made of a piece of well-seasoned hickory plank. The plank is steamed in a wash boiler or other large kettle and then bent to a nice curve, as shown in *Figure 1*. It is held in this curve until dry, with two pieces nailed on the sides, as shown.

After the piece is thoroughly dried out, remove the sidepieces and cut into sections with a saw, as shown in *Figure 2*. The pieces are then dressed round. A piece of plank 12 in. wide and 2 ft. long will make six boomerangs.

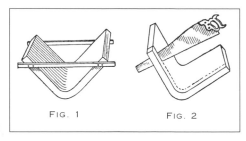

FIG. 1   FIG. 2

BENDING AND CUTTING THE WOOD.

To throw a boomerang, grasp and hold it the same as a club, with the hollow side away from you. Practice first at some object about 25 ft. distant, and in a short time you will be able to hit the mark over 100 ft. away. Any worker in wood can turn out a great number of boomerangs cheaply.

STOCKING *the* SHOP

— AN EMERGENCY SOLDERING TOOL —

Occasionally one finds a piece of soldering to do that is impossible to reach with even the smallest of ordinary soldering irons or coppers. Find a length of copper wire as large as the job will permit and sufficiently long to admit being bent at one end to form a rough handle. File or dress to a point on the other end, and heat and tin exactly as a regular copper wire would be treated. The work will cause no trouble on account of inaccessibility and no dismantling of walls is necessary.

— A SMALL BENCH LATHE MADE OF PIPE FITTINGS —

The most important machine in use in the modern machine or woodworking shop is the lathe. The uses to which this wonderful machine can be put are too numerous to describe, but there is hardly a mechanical operation in which the turning lathe does not figure. For this reason, every amateur mechanic and woodworker who has a workshop, no matter how small, is anxious to possess a lathe of some sort. A good and substantial homemade lathe that is suitable for wood turning and light metalwork may be constructed from pipe and pipe fittings, as shown in the accompanying sketch.

The bed of this lathe is made of a piece of 1-in. pipe about 30 in. long. It can be made longer or shorter, but if it is made much longer, a larger size of pipe should be used. The headstock is made of two tees joined by a standard long nipple, as shown in *Figure 1*. All the joints should be screwed up tight and then fastened with 3/16-in. pins to keep them from turning. The ends of the bed are fixed to the baseboard by means of elbows, nipples, and flanges, arranged as shown. The two bearings in the headstock are of brass; the spindle hole should be drilled and reamed after they are screwed in place in the tee. The spindle should be of steel and long enough to reach through the bearing and pulley and still have enough end left for the center point. The point should extend

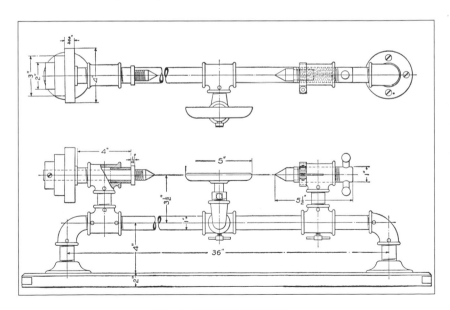

FIG. 1: DETAILS OF LATHE.

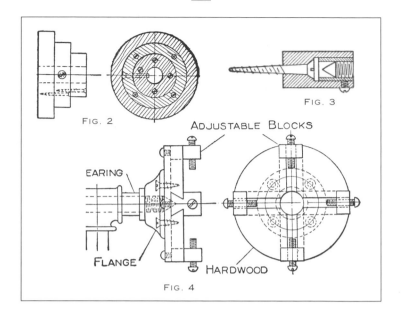

FIG. 2

FIG. 3

ADJUSTABLE BLOCKS

EARING

FLANGE

HARDWOOD

FIG. 4

about 1½ in. out from the collar. The collar can be turned or shrunk on the spindle as desired. The end of the spindle should be threaded to receive a chuck.

The tailstock is also made of two tees joined by a nipple. The lower tee should be bored out for a sliding fit on the bed pipe. The upper one should be tapped with a machine tap for the spindle that is threaded to fit it. The spindle has a handle fitted at one end and has the other end bored out for the tailstock center. Both the tailstock and the headstock center points should be hardened. A clamp for holding the tailstock spindle is made of a piece of strap iron, bent and drilled as shown. It is held together by means of a small machine screw and a knurled nut. The tee should have a slot cut in it about one-half its length, and it should also have one bead filed away so that the clamp will fit tightly over it.

The handrest is made from a tapering elbow, a tee, and a forging. The forging can be made by a machinist at a small expense. Both the lower tees of the handrest and the tailstock should be provided with screw clamps to hold them in place.

The pulley is made of hardwood pieces ¾ to 1 in. thick, as desired. It is fastened to the spindle by means of a screw, as shown in *Figure 2*; a key can be used as well.

Care must be taken to get the tailstock center vertically over the bed or else taper turning will result. To do this, a straight line should be scratched on the top of the bed pipe, and when the tailstock is set exactly vertical, a corresponding line

is made on this. This will save a great deal of time and trouble and possibly some errors.

The two designs of chucks shown in *Figures 3* and *4* are very easy to make and will answer for a great variety of work.

As the details are clearly shown and the general dimensions given on the accompanying sketches, it should not be a difficult matter for the young mechanic to construct this machine.

— How to Make a Rabbet Plane —

A rabbet plane is very little used by mechanics, but when it is wanted for a piece of work, it is wanted badly. While doing an unusual piece of work, a woodworker needed a rabbet plane. Having none, he made a plane as shown in the sketch in less time than it would have taken to go out and borrow one.

The body of the plane was made of a piece of 2 x 4 in.

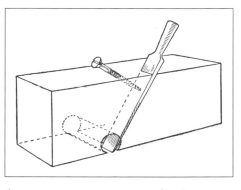

A PLANE MADE OF A PIECE OF 2 X 4 IN. PINE, A CHISEL, AND A LARGE WOOD SCREW.

pine, 1 ft. long. A 1-in. chisel was used for the bit. A place was marked on one side of the wood to be cut out for the chisel, and a 1-in. hole bored through, the narrow way, so that one edge of the bit cut through the bottom, forming a

slit for the edge of the chisel. After cutting a groove for the chisel blade and turning in a long wood screw, as shown, to hold the chisel in place, he had as good a rabbet plane as could be purchased.

— A BACKSTOP FOR A WORKBENCH —

In planing small pieces on a bench, they usually have a tendency to tip up or slide around. This difficulty can be easily overcome by providing the bench with an extra backstop. For this purpose a discarded plane iron will do very well. Its edge

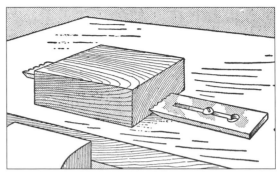

A PLANE BIT FASTENED TO THE TOP OF A BENCH
TO HOLD BLOCKS WHILE PLANING THEM.

should be notched so that it will easily enter the wood. The edges of its central slot should be beveled off if an ordinary wood screw is used to fasten it to the bench. A series of holes several inches apart and in line with the regular backstop should be bored into the bench so that the screw and iron can be readily changed to fit varying lengths.

— A VISE USED AS A CALIPER GAUGE —

Not infrequently it is desired to know the distance from one side to another of some part that cannot be directly measured with a rule, and when no calipers are at hand. But with a vise handy, the measurement can be made with ease and with sufficient accuracy for all practical purposes, if the vise is not too worn. This trick is particularly adapted for callipering threaded

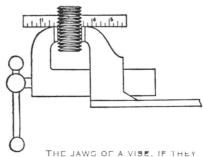

THE JAWS OF A VISE, IF THEY
ARE TRUE, WILL MAKE A CALIPER
GAUGE GIVING A PERFECT
MEASUREMENT.

parts, as threads cannot be measured readily with ordinary calipers. How this may be done is shown in the sketch, which illustrates the method as applied to a screw. The work is gripped between the jaws of the vise, and the opening then measured with a rule.

— HOMEMADE CARPENTER'S VISE —

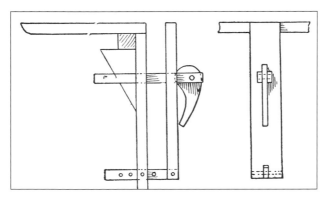

VISE MADE ENTIRELY OF WOOD.

The sketch illustrates an easily made, quick-working wood vise that has proved very satisfactory in the workshop. The customary screw is replaced by an open bar held on one end by a wedge-shaped block, and the excess taken up on the opposite end by an eccentric lever. The wedge is worked by a string passing through the top of the bench, and should be weighted on the other end to facilitate the automatic downward movement.

The capacity of the vise, of course, depends on the size and shape of the wedge-shaped block.

— A HANDY DRILL GAUGE —

The accompanying sketch shows a simple drill gauge that will be found very handy by amateurs. The gauge consists of a piece of hardwood, ¾ in. thick, with a width and length that will be suitable for the size and number of drills you have on hand. Drill a hole through the wood with

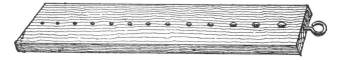

DRILL GAUGE.

each drill you have, and place a screw eye in one end, to be used as a hanger. When you want to drill a hole for a pipe, bolt, screw, etc., you use the gauge to determine what size drill must be used in drilling the hole.

— A DOWEL-TURNING TOOL —

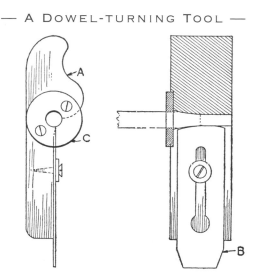

THE TOOL IS VERY SIMILAR TO A PLANE AND IS USED WITH A LATHE FOR TURNING DOWELS.

The owner of a wood or metal lathe can easily construct a tool that will turn dowels of any size quickly. This tool consists of a block of wood, shaped as shown at *A*, and a plane bit, *B*, attached with a wood screw. The hole in the collet, *C*, must be sized to admit the rough stock freely but also prevent it from wobbling as the stick turns. The stock is chucked in the ordinary manner, and the tool is run on the outer end.

— How to Make a Wing Nut —

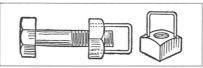

Finding that he needed some wing nuts and not being able to purchase them in the size he wanted, a machinist made them from ordinary nuts. A hole was drilled through opposite corners of each nut, and a staple made of wire was riveted in the holes, as shown in the sketch. The staple should be long enough to admit the end of the bolt.

— How to Make a Cheap Bracket Saw —

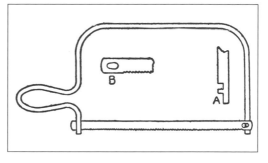

For the frame use ⅜-in. round iron, bending it as shown in the diagram and filing a knob on each end on which to hook the blade. For the blade an old clock spring will do nicely. Heat the spring enough to take some of the temper out of it. This will allow you to drill the holes in the ends, as shown, and file in the teeth. Make the blade 12 in. long, with 10 teeth to the inch. *A* and *B* show how the blade fits on the frame.

— Homemade Workbench —

The first appliance necessary for the boy's workshop is a workbench. The average boy who desires to construct his own apparatus can make the bench as described here. Four pieces of 2 x 4 in. pine are cut 23 in. long for the legs, and a tenon made on each end of them, ½ in. thick, 3½ in. wide, and 1½ in. long, as shown at *A* and *B*, *Figure 1*. The crosspieces at the top and bottom of the legs are made from the same material, and cut 20 in. long. A mortise is made 1¼ in. from each end of these pieces and in the narrow edge of them, as shown at *C* and *D*, *Figure 1*. The corners are then cut sloping from the edge of the leg out and to the middle of the piece, as shown. When each pair of legs is fitted to a pair of crosspieces, they will form the two supports for the bench. These supports are held together and braced with two braces, or connecting pieces of 2 x 4 in. pine, 24 in. long. The joints are made between the ends of these pieces and the legs by boring a hole through each leg and into the center of each end of the braces, to a depth of 4 in., as shown at *J*, *Figure 2*. On the back side of the braces, bore holes intersecting the other holes for a place to insert the nut of a bolt, as shown at *H*. Four ⅜ x 6 in. bolts are placed in the holes bored, and the joints are drawn together as shown at *J*. The ends of the two braces must be sawed off perfectly square to make the supports stand up straight.

In making this part of the bench, be sure to have the joints fit closely and to draw the bolts up tight on the stretchers. There is nothing quite so annoying as to have the bench support sway while work is being done on its top. It would be wise to add a cross brace on the back side to prevent any rocking while planing

boards if the bench is to be used for large work.

The main top board *M*, *Figure 2*, may be made from one piece of 2 x 12 in. plank, 3½ ft. long, or made up of 14 strips of maple, ⅞ in. thick by 2 in. wide by 3½ ft. long, set on edge, each strip glued and screwed to its neighbor. When building up a top like this, be careful to put the strips together with the grain running in the same direction so that the top may be planed smooth. The back board *N* is the same length as the main top board *M*, 8½ in. wide and only ⅞ in. thick. It is fitted into a ½-in. rabbet in back of board *M*. These boards form the top of the bench and are fastened to the top pieces of the supports with long screws. The board *E* is 10 in. wide and nailed to the back of the bench. On top of this board and at right angles to it is fastened a 2½ in. board, *F*. These two boards are ⅞ in. thick and 3½ ft. long. Holes are bored or notches are cut in the projecting board, *F*, to hold tools.

Details of the vise are shown in *Figure 3*, which is composed of a 2 x 6 in. block 12 in. long, into which is fastened an iron bench screw, *S*. Two ⅞ x 1½ in. guide rails, *G*, 20 in. long, are fastened into mortises of the block, as shown at *K*, and they slide in corresponding mortises in a piece

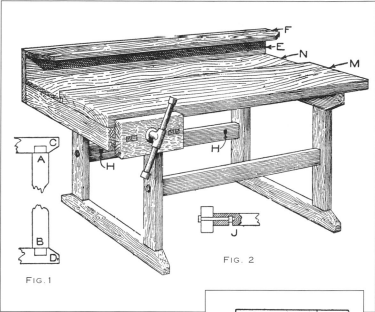

FIG. 1

FIG. 2

FIG. 3

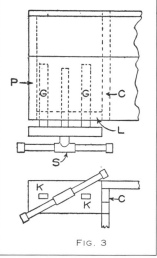

DETAILS OF CONSTRUCTION OF
HOMEMADE WORKBENCH.

of 2 x 4 in. pine bolted to the underside of the main top board, as shown at *L*. The bench screw nut is fastened into the 2 x 4 in. piece, *L*, between the two mortised holes. *L* is securely nailed to one of the support's top crosspieces, *C*, and to a piece of 2 x 4 in. pine, *P*, that is bolted to the undersides of the top boards at the end of the bench. The bolts and the bench screw can be purchased from any hardware store at minimal cost.

— Bench Stop for Planing Thin Boards —

A bench stop for planing thin boards with a hand plane may be made in the following manner: Procure a piece of strap iron about ¼ in. thick, 1½ to 2 in. wide, and about 6 in. long. File or grind one edge sharp on top, and drill a ¼-in. hole through the center. Cut a slot in a board or in the workbench large enough to receive the stop *A* flat. Place enough strips of rubber or fit two coil springs, *B*, to raise the sharp edge out of the slot. Insert a screw in

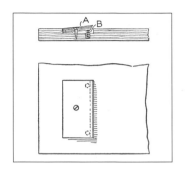

the hole of the stop, and adjust it to the desired height by turning the screw up or down.

— A Workbench for the Amateur —

The accompanying detail drawing shows a design for a portable workbench suitable for the amateur woodworker. This bench can be made easily by anyone who has a few sharp tools and a little spare time. If the stock is purchased from the mill already planed and cut to length, much of the hard labor will be saved. Birch or maple wood makes a very good bench. The following pieces should be ordered:

- four legs, 3 x 3 x 36 in.
- two side rails, 3 x 3 x 62½ in.
- two end rails, 3 x 3 x 20 in.

- one back board, 1 x 9 x 80 in.
- one top board, 2 x 12 x 77 in.
- one top board, 1 x 12 x 77 in.
- two crosspieces, 1½ x 3 x 24 in.
- one piece for clamp, 1½ x 6½ x 12 in.
- one piece for clamp, 1½ x 6½ x 14 in.
- four guides, 2 x 2 x 18 in.
- one screw block, 3 x 3 x 6 in.
- one piece, 1½ x 4½ x 10½ in.

Make the lower frame first. Cut tenons on the rails and mortise the posts, then fasten them securely together with ⅜ x 5 in. lag screws,

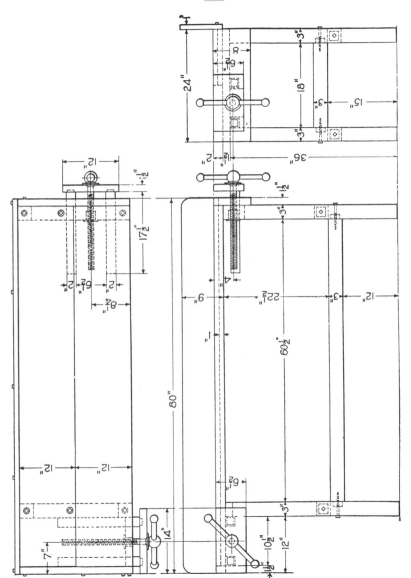

DETAILS OF THE BENCH.

COMPLETED WORKBENCH.

as shown. Also fasten the 1½ x 3 x 24 in. pieces to the tops of the posts with screws. The heads should be countersunk for the holes bored in the top boards to fit over them. Fasten the front top board to the crosspieces with lag screws through from the underside. The screws can be put in from the top for the 1-in.-thick top board.

Fasten the endpieces on with screws, countersinking the heads of the vise end. Cut 2-in.-square holes in the 1½ x 4½ x 10½ in. pieces for the vise slides, and fit it in place for the side vise. Also cut square holes in the one endpiece for the end vise slides, as shown. Now fit up the two clamps. Fasten the slides to the front pieces with screws. Countersink the heads

of the screws so that they will not be in the way of the hands when the vise is used. The two clamp screws should be about 1½ in. in diameter. They can be purchased at a hardware store. A block should be fitted under the crosspiece to hold the nut for the end vise. After you have the slides fitted, put them in place, and bore the holes for the clamp screws.

The back board can now be fastened to the back with screws, as shown in the top view. The bench is now complete, except for the couple of coats of oil that should be applied to give it a finish and preserve the wood. The amateur workman, as well as the pattern maker, will find this a very handy and serviceable bench for his workshop.

As the amateur workman does not always know just what tools he will need, a list is given that will answer for a general class of work. This list can be added to as the workman becomes more proficient in his line and has need for other tools. If each tool is kept in a certain place, it can be easily found when wanted.

- one bench plane or jointer
- one jack plane or smoother
- one crosscut saw, 24 in.
- one ripsaw, 24 in.
- one claw hammer
- one set of gimlets
- one brace and set of bits
- two screwdrivers, 3 and 6 in.
- one countersink
- one compass saw
- one set of chisels
- one wood scraper
- one monkey wrench
- one 2-ft. rule
- one marking gauge
- one pair of pliers
- one nail set
- one pair of dividers
- one pocket level
- one 6-in. try square
- one oilstone
- No. 1, 2, and 00 sandpaper

— A HOMEMADE HAND VISE —

A very useful little hand vise can easily be made from a hinge and a bolt carrying a wing nut. Get a fast joint hinge about 2 in. or more long and a bolt about ½ in. long that will fit the holes in the hinge. Put the bolt through the middle hole of the hinge, and replace the nut as shown in the drawing. With this device, any small object may be firmly held by simply placing it between the sides of the hinge and tightening the nut.

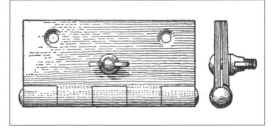

HAND VISE MADE FROM A HINGE.

— A Staple Puller —

A very simple way to pull a staple is to use the claws of an ordinary carpenter's hammer and a nail, as shown in the sketch. The staple can be removed quickly without being bent, and no damage to the material into which it was driven will result.

— Wire Mesh Used as a Shelf —

In covering a window back of a lathe with wire mesh for protection, one homeowner also made a shelf for the tools between the windowsill and the lathe bed, using the same material. The mesh used was ¼ in. The shelf always stays clean, as the shavings and dirt fall through, and the tools may be readily picked up.

— A Homemade Carpenter's Gauge —

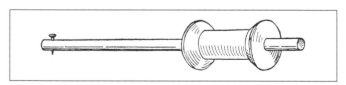

ROUND STICK IN A SPOOL.

The home workshop can be supplied with a carpenter's gauge without any expense by the use of a large spool and a round stick of wood. The stick should be dressed to fit the hole in the spool snugly, and a small brad driven through one end so that the point will protrude about 1/16 in.

The adjustment of the gauge is secured by driving the stick in the hole in the direction desired. A better way, and one that will make the adjusting easy, is to file the point end of a screw eye flat and use it as a set-screw through a hole in the side of the spool.

— A Centering Gauge —

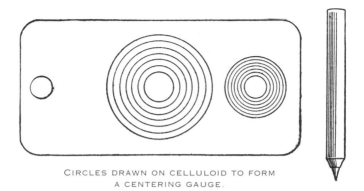

CIRCLES DRAWN ON CELLULOID TO FORM
A CENTERING GAUGE.

The centering gauge consists of a piece of celluloid on which several circles are drawn, having different diameters but all drawn from the same center. A small hole is made at the center to admit the point of a center punch. Two sets of circles may be drawn on one piece, as shown, but the lines should be spaced far enough apart to allow the metal to be clearly seen through the celluloid. The sheet is placed on the end of a shaft and adjusted so that a ring will match the circumference of the shaft, then the center punch is set in the center hole and struck with a hammer. The center punch for marking is shown in the sketch.

— How to Make a Lathe —

A small speed lathe suitable for turning wood or small metal articles may be easily made at very little expense. A lathe of this kind is shown in the illustration, *Figure 1*, where *A* is the headstock, *B* the bed, and *C* the tailstock. The workman who first built this lathe runs the lathe by power, using an electric motor and countershaft. But it could be run by foot power, if desired. A large cone pulley would then be required, but this may be made in the same manner as the small one, which will be described later.

The bed of the machine is made of wood, as shown in *Figures 2* and *3*, hardwood being preferable for this

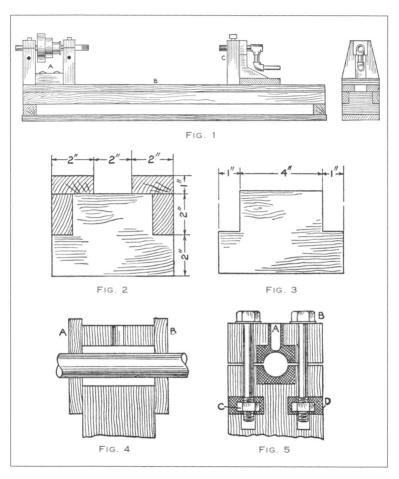

FIG. 1

FIG. 2

FIG. 3

FIG. 4

FIG. 5

ASSEMBLED LATHE BED AND BEARING DETAILS.

purpose. *Figure 2* shows an end view of the assembled bed, and *Figure 3* shows how the ends are cut out to receive the sidepieces.

The headstock, *Figure 6*, is fastened to the bed by means of carriage bolts, *A*, which pass through a piece of wood, *B*, on the underside of the

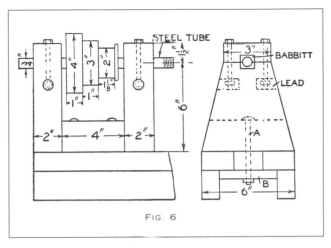

FIG. 6

HEADSTOCK DETAILS.

bed. The shaft is made of ¾-in. steel tubing about ⅛ in. thick, and runs in Babbitt bearings, one of which is shown in *Figure 5*.

To make these bearings, cut a square hole in the wood, as shown, making half of the square in each half of the bearing. Separate the two halves of the bearing slightly by placing a piece of cardboard on each side, just touching the shaft. The edges that touch the shaft should be notched like the teeth of a saw so as to allow the Babbitt to run into the lower half of the bearing. The notches for this purpose may be about ⅛ in. in pitch and ⅛ in. deep. Place pieces of wood against the ends of the bearing,

as shown at *A* and *B*, *Figure 4*, and drill a hole in the top of the bearing, as shown in *Figure 4*.

The bearing is then ready to be poured. Have a machinist or similar professional do this. He should heat the Babbitt well, but not hot enough to burn it. It is wise to have the shaft hot, too, so that the Babbitt will not be chilled when it strikes the shaft. If the shaft is thoroughly chalked or smoked, the Babbitt will not stick to it. After pouring, the professional should remove the shaft and split the bearing with a round, tapered wooden pin. If the bearing has been properly made, it will split along the line of the notched cardboard where

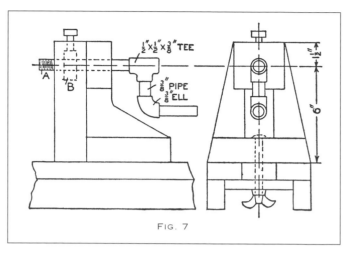

FIG. 7

DETAILS OF TAILSTOCK.

the section of the metal is smallest. Then you can drill a hole in the top, as shown at *A*, *Figure 5*, drilling just deep enough to have the point of the drill appear at the lower side. This cavity acts as an oil cup and prevents the bearing from running dry.

The bolts, *B*, *Figure 5*, are passed through holes in the wood and screwed into the nuts *C*, which are let into the holes *D*, the holes afterward being filled with melted Babbitt, poured by a professional. This type of bearing will be found very satisfactory and may be used to advantage on other machines.

After the bearings are completed the cone pulley can be placed on the shaft. To make this pulley, cut three circular pieces of wood to the dimensions given in *Figure 6*, and fasten these together with nails and glue. If not perfectly true, they may be turned up after assembling by rigging up a temporary tool rest in front of the headstock.

The tailstock, *Figure 7*, is fastened to the bed in the same manner as the headstock, except that thumb nuts are used on the carriage bolts, thus allowing the tailstock to be shifted when necessary. The mechanism of the center holder is obtained by using a ½-in. pipe, *A*, and a ½-in. lock nut, *B*, embedded in the wood.

— HOMEMADE SCROLL SAW —

A scroll saw, if used once, becomes indispensable in any home carpenter's chest. Yet it is safe to say that not one in ten contains it. A scroll saw is much more useful than a keyhole saw for sawing small and irregular holes. Many fancy knick-knacks, such as brackets, bookracks, and shelves, can be made with one.

A simple yet serviceable scroll-saw frame can be made from a piece of cold-rolled steel rod $3/32$ or $\frac{1}{4}$ in. in diameter, two $\frac{1}{8}$-in. machine screws, four washers, and four square nuts. The rod should be 36 to 38 in. long, bent as shown in *Figure 1*. Place one washer on each screw, and put the screws through the eyelets *A*, then place other washers on and fasten in place by screwing one nut on each screw, clamping the washers against the frame as tightly as possible. The blade, which can be purchased at a local hardware store, is fastened between the clamping nut and another nut, as shown in the bottom detail.

If two wing nuts having the same number and size of threads are available, use them in place of the outside nuts. They are easier to turn when inserting a saw blade in a hole or when removing broken blades.

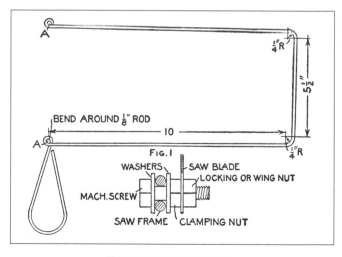

FRAME MADE OF A ROD.

— HOMEMADE LEVEL —

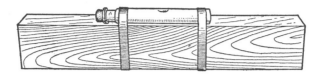

Having need of a level and there being no place to obtain one within several miles, a workman constructed one as follows: A long medicine bottle was filled with water and tied to a straight piece of wood, 2 ft. long. After setting it properly by turning the piece end for end several times, he found that it could be used with accuracy.

— CABINET FOR THE
AMATEUR'S WORKSHOP —

One of the most convenient adjuncts to an amateur's work-bench is a cabinet of some sort in which to keep nails, rivets, screws, etc., instead of leaving them scattered all about the bench. An easily made cabinet for this purpose is shown in the accompanying illustration. The case may be made of ½-in. white pine, or white wood of a suitable size to hold the required number of drawers, which slide on strips of the same material, cut and dressed ½ in. square. The drawers are made of empty cigar boxes of uniform size, which, if one is not a smoker, may be readily obtained from any cigar dealer, as they are usually thrown away when empty.

Small knobs may be added if desired, but these are not necessary, because the spaces between the drawers will leave ample room to grasp them with the fingers. Labels of some kind are needed, and one of the neatest things for this purpose is the embossed aluminum label, such as is stamped by the well-known penny-in-the-slot machines to be found in many railroad stations and amusement places.

{CHAPTER 5}

RECYCLE *and* REPURPOSE

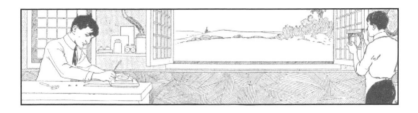

NEW USES *for* OLD THINGS

— GARDEN HOSE MAKES WINDOW SQUEEGEE —

An old broom handle and a piece of garden hose can be made into a squeegee for scraping the water from windows without the necessity of wiping the glass with cloths. It can also be used for scraping water and slush from sidewalks. A piece of the broom handle is cut to a semicircular section and covered with a piece of garden hose that has been split in half and tacked to the wood. A suitable handle, as shown in the drawing, completes the tool.

— NEW LIFE IN THE GARDEN FOR SPENT MARKER PENS —

Don't discard your dried-out felt-tip pens. The pens can still serve a function if you use them to hold the seed packets to mark the plantings in your garden. Leave the marker in place until plants are identifiable.

— INEXPENSIVE CHRISTMAS DECORATIONS —

Decorating your home for the Christmas season need not be an expensive proposition if you utilize materials that, in most homes, are already at hand. For instance, to letter greetings on door and windowpanes, use a thick paste of flour and water. Sprinkle coarse salt over the lettering while still wet, and the result will be an appropriate frosty appearance. If desired, greatly magnified snowflakes can be taped to the panes around the lettering. These are provided in realistic designs simply by cutting out sections of intricately patterned paper doilies. On windows fitted with venetian blinds, a novel effect will be attained by pasting or taping a large seasonal picture to one side of the blind when the slats are closed and cutting the picture in strips by drawing a razor blade along the edge of each slat. When the blind is open, the picture will not be visible, but a pull of the slat cord brings it suddenly into view. Pinecones always can be counted on to help supply a Yuletide atmosphere and can be used in a number of ways. But first, brighten them up by brushing with rubber cement and then sprinkling liberally with metallic powders. Tie the cones to the Christmas tree with ribbons, use them in making wreaths, or fasten three or four of the cones together to form a holder for candles. And if you wish some giant-size candles, make them by placing regular candles vertically in tin cans and then filling the latter with melted paraffin. When the paraffin has hardened, cut the bottoms out of the cans to make the giant candles easy to remove. If you use milk cartons as molds, square candles can be made in the same way. Colorful miniature Christmas trees are made by inserting long knitting needles through the centers of paper plates and slipping tree-ornament balls over the needles. Place the largest balls at the bottoms of the needles, and graduate them in size to the tops. Adorn the edges of the plates with crinkled foil paper or lace from a doily. The names of family members and guests, printed in befitting colors on the dinner dishes or glassware, will serve as a unique way to place the diners and at the same time add to the spirit of festivity. Use red nail polish for the lettering, and trim it with clear nail polish tinted green by adding food coloring.

— CLAY FLOWERPOTS USED FOR BIRDHOUSES —

Novel use of the common garden flowerpot may be made by enlarging the small opening at the bottom with a pair of pliers and carefully breaking the clay away until the opening is large enough to admit a small bird.

POTS FASTENED TO A BOARD FOR USE AS A BIRDHOUSE.

Place the pot, bottom side up, on a board 3 in. wider than the diameter of the largest pot used. Fasten it to the board with wood cleats and brass screws. Fit the cleats as close as possible to the sides of the pot. One or more pots may be used, as shown in the sketch.

The board on which the pots are fastened is nailed or screwed to a post or pole 10 or 12 ft. in height. The board is braced with lath or similar strips of wood, making a framework suitable for a roost. In designing the roost, the lath can be arranged to make it quite attractive, or the braces may be of twigs and branches to make a rustic effect.

— A FISH-SCALING KNIFE —

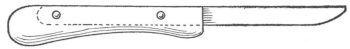

SCALING KNIFE.

A useful fish-scaling and -skinning knife can be made of an old broken hacksaw blade. This must be at least 6 in. long and will make a knife with a 3-in. blade. Grind the blade to the shape shown and make a handle for it by using two strips of maple, ¼ in. thick and 4 in. long. These are riveted together with 3 in. of the blade between them.

— NEW USE FOR A VACUUM CLEANER —

An amateur mechanic who had been much annoyed by the insects that were attracted to his electric lights found a solution in the pneumatic moth trap described in an issue of *Popular Mechanics*. He fixed a funnel to the end of the intake tube of a vacuum cleaner and hung it under a globe. The insects came to the light, circled over the funnel, and disappeared. He captured several pounds' worth in a few hours.

— NEW USE FOR BROKEN WOODEN CHAIRS —

Don't destroy an old wooden chair or stool; it's still worth something other than kindling wood. For example, it can be used as a hose rack, as you see in the photo. And what can you find other than a commercial hose reel to serve this purpose better? Such a rack, made by cutting the back off an old chair and screwing it to the wall, holds 50 to 100 ft. of hose without kinks.

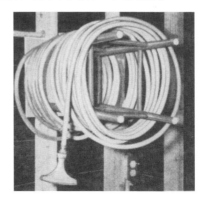

— ATTACHING RUNNERS TO A BICYCLE FOR WINTER USE —

Instead of storing away your bicycle for the winter, attach runners and use it on the ice. The runners can be made from ¼ x 1 in. iron and fastened to the bicycle frame as shown in the sketch. The tire is removed from the rim of the rear wheel and large screws turned into the

BICYCLE FITTED WITH RUNNERS FOR SNOW.

rim, leaving the greater part of the screw extending. Cut off the heads of the screws and file them to a point. The rear runners should be set so that the rim of the wheel will be about ½ in. above the runner level.

— GLASS BOTTLE AS A CANDLE LAMP —

A candle may be carried in a glass bottle, as shown in the sketch, with little danger of setting fire to surrounding objects and without permitting the melted wax to leak upon the floor. The bottom of the bottle is cut off and the candle inserted as shown, the neck affording a convenient handle.

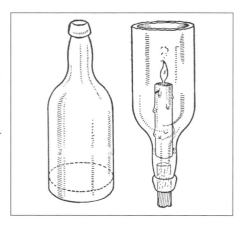

— BAIT NET MADE FROM AN UMBRELLA —

An easily carried minnow net that will fit into a small space can be made from a discarded umbrella frame. Cut fine meshed bobbinet to fit the ribs of the frame, using linen fish line as thread to sew the net to the frame. The handle is removed, and a fairly heavy cord is tied to the shaft of the umbrella when seining for minnows.

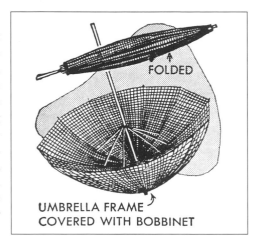

FOLDED

UMBRELLA FRAME
COVERED WITH BOBBINET

— KNIFE MADE FROM A HACKSAW BLADE —

A very serviceable knife with excellent cutting qualities can be made easily from a discarded hacksaw blade. The dimensions given in the sketch make a knife of convenient size.

The saw teeth are ground off on an emery wheel or grindstone to a smooth edge, parallel with the back edge. For the handle, take two pieces of hardwood, dressing one surface of each piece, and cut a groove as wide

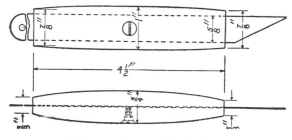

DETAILS OF KNIFE HANDLE.

and thick as the saw blade. Place the blade in the groove, and glue the two dressed sides of the wood together. After the glue has dried, the blade can be pulled out of the groove and the wood shaped to any desired form.

A small wood screw is put through one side of the handle to prevent the blade from sliding. After completing the handle, the blade is put back into the groove and sharpened to a cutting edge.

— WOODEN COAT HANGER PROVIDES SHORT RAILS FOR WORKBENCH OR TABLETOP —

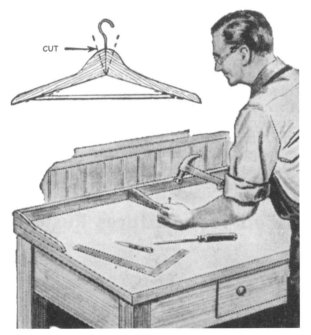

CUT

The arms of a wooden coat hanger are already shaped in such a way as to provide short rails for the top of a workbench or table. It's just a matter of cutting the arms from the hanger, as shown, and fastening them in place. A wooden backing strip should be nailed to the edge of the bench top before attaching the rails.

— A Traveler's Shaving Mug —

Take an ordinary collapsible drinking cup and place a cake of shaving soap in the bottom ring. This will provide a shaving mug always ready for the traveler and one that will occupy very little space in the grip.

— Use for Paper Bags —

When groceries are delivered, save the paper bags and use them for storing bread and cakes. Tie the neck of the bag with a string and it will keep the contents fresh and clean.

Tin Can Alley

— Cheese Grater and Ashtray Made from a Tin Can —

Being in need of a cheese grater and finding it inconvenient to go many miles into town, a handy young man constructed a satisfactory makeshift. He took a heavily tinned can and cut it in two, as shown in the sketch. By punching holes through it from the inside, a practical grater resulted. From the remaining half of the can he made an ashtray, as shown. The semicircular ends were bent over to form a rest, and by cutting portions at the sides and bending them in, a convenient rest for a pipe or cigar was afforded.

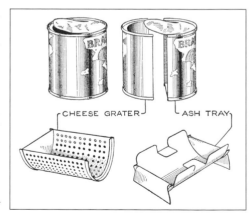

NECESSITY RESULTED IN THE MAKING OF A CHEESE GRATER AND ASHTRAY FROM A TIN CAN.

— NAIL CARRIER MADE OF CANS —

Four ordinary tin cans fastened to a wooden block, as shown in the illustration, make a serviceable and practical carrier for nails, staples, or similar materials used in making repairs on the farm or in the shop. The tops of the cans are cut out carefully, and the edges smoothed off so as not to injure the hand in removing nails from them. The tops are cut to the shape shown, attached to the block, and the contrivance provided with a handle, making it convenient to carry. If cans are used having covers that may be pried off,

the central block should be extended and the handle nailed to it.

— OUTDOOR LANTERN MADE OF A TIN CAN —

Campers, and others who have need of an emergency lantern—or even backyard night enthusiasts who want light for parties or other gatherings—may be interested in a contrivance shown in the sketch, which was used in preference to other lanterns and made quickly when no light was at hand. It consists of an ordinary tin can in the side of which a candle has been fixed. A ring of holes was punched through the metal around the candle, and wires were placed at the opposite side for

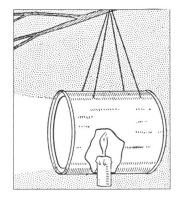

support. The glistening interior of the can reflects the light admirably.

— Tin Can Candleholder —

The candlestick or holder shown in the illustration is made of an ordinary tin can such as is used for canning salmon or potted ham. Three triangular cuts are made in the cover or bottom of the can, and the points turned up about the candle. The can may be bronzed, silvered, enameled, or otherwise decorated, thus making it ornamental as well as useful.

— Potatoes Baked in Tin Can Ovens While on Camping Trips —

When potatoes are baked in a campfire, considerable time is usually required, as it is best practice not to put the potatoes in until the fire has burned down to provide hot coals. However, if you want to hasten the cooking process, baking can be accomplished quickly by placing the potatoes under inverted tin cans and then building the fire over the cans. Thus the cans serve as small temporary ovens.

— BOY SCOUT LANTERN MADE FROM TIN CANS USES CANDLE TO PROVIDE LIGHT SOURCE —

Taking one of these candle-burning lanterns on your next overnight camping trip will furnish extra light without wasting flashlight batteries. In addition to costing practically nothing, the lightweight lantern is easily carried, and the candle is well protected from wind and rain. The lantern is made from two tin cans, one of them providing a base, and the other, which is mounted horizontally, serving as a reflector to give a spotlight effect. The can forming the base is cut away so that the other will fit neatly within its sides, and the two cans are soldered together. The candle is held upright in the reflector by impaling it on a short nail that is driven through the side of the can and soldered in place. A wire handle is fastened to the top of the lantern by means of a metal tab soldered near each end of the can. If an opening is cut in the side of the base can, spare candles and dry matches can be carried inside the lantern. This opening can be fitted with a metal cover.

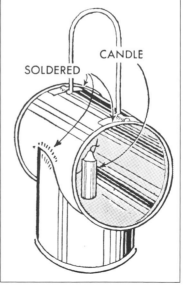

SOLDERED

CANDLE

Piping Up

— More Uses for Pipe Fittings —

It would seem that the number of useful articles that can be made from pipes and fittings is unlimited. The sketch shows two more that may be added to the list. *A* and *B* are front and side views of a lamp screen, and *C* is a dumbbell. The lampshade is particularly useful for shading the eyes when reading or writing and, if enameled white on

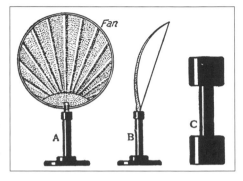

LAMPSHADE AND DUMBBELL.

the concave side, makes an excellent reflector for drawing at night or for microscopic work.

The standard and base, consisting of an ordinary pipe flange bushed down to receive the upright nipple, are enameled a jet black. If the device is to be used on a polished table, a piece of felt should be glued to the bottom. A good way to hold the fan

in the nipple is to use a small wedge.

The dumbbells are made of short pieces of ¾-in. pipe with 1- to 2-in. couplings fastened to each end by pouring in a quick-setting metal-to-metal epoxy adhesive in the space between the pipes and the couplings. The appearance is greatly improved by enameling black, and, if desired, the handles may be covered with leather.

— Pipe Fittings Form Sturdy Clothes Pole for Closet —

Unlike the wooden clothes pole that bends and creaks under the weight of winter garments, this pipe rack will handle your heaviest

garments safely. Its strength is limited only by that of the shelf to which it is attached. The original rack was made up of 1-in. pipe and

fittings, although ½- or ¾-in. pipe can be used. As shown in the drawing, the lengths of pipe that form the clothes pole are suspended from the underside of the closet shelf with floor flanges and nipples, the latter being about 2½ in. long. The nipples are turned into an elbow at each end of the clothes pole and into one or more pipe tees used to join the pipe sections. The rack is completely assembled before the flanges are screwed to the underside of the shelf.

— HANDSLED MADE OF PIPE AND FITTINGS —

The accompanying sketch shows how an ordinary handsled can be made of ¾-in. pipe and fittings. Each runner is made of one piece of pipe bent to the proper shape. This can be accomplished by

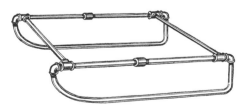

HANDSLED PARTS MADE OF PIPE FITTINGS.

filling the pipe with melted rosin, then bending to the shape desired, and afterward removing the rosin by heating. Each joint is turned up tightly and well pinned or brazed. One of the top crosspieces should have right-hand and left-hand threads, or be fitted with a union. Also, one of the top pieces connecting the rear part to the front part of each runner must be fitted in the same way. The top is fastened to the two crosspieces. Such a handsled can be made in a few hours' time and, when complete, is much better than a wood sled.

— Handcar Made of Pipe and Fittings —

Although apparently complicated, the construction of the miniature handcar shown in the accompanying illustration is very simple. With a few exceptions, all the parts are short lengths of pipe and common tees, elbows, and nipples.

The wheels were manufactured for use on a baby carriage; the sprocket wheel and chain were taken from a discarded bicycle, which was also drawn upon for the cork handle used on the steering lever. The floor is made from 1-in. white pine, 14 in. wide and 48 in. long, to which are bolted ordinary flanges to hold the framing and the propelling and steering apparatus together; the axles were made from ⅜-in. shafting. The fifth wheel consists of two small flanges working on the face surfaces. These flanges and the auxiliary steering rod are connected to the axles by means of

BOY'S HANDCAR.

holes stamped in the piece of sheet iron, which encases the axle. The sheet iron was first properly stamped and then bent around the axle. The levers for propelling and steering the car work in fulcrums made for use in lever valves; the turned wooden handles by which these levers are operated were inserted through holes drilled in the connecting tees. The working joint for the steering and hand levers consists of a ½ x ⅜ x ⅜ in. tee, a ½ x ⅜ in. cross, and a piece of rod threaded on both ends and screwed into the tee. The cross is reamed and, with the rod, forms a bearing.

The operation of this little hand-car is very similar in principle to that of the ordinary tricycle. The machine can be propelled as fast as a boy can run. It responds readily to the slightest movement of the steering lever.

TIRED *of* WASTE

— TIRE PROVIDES RUBBER "HORSESHOES" WHEN GAME IS PLAYED INDOORS —

Especially suitable for indoor play, this game of horseshoes is ideal entertainment for children on rainy days. Because the "shoes" are rubber, being cut from an old car tire, they cannot scratch the floor and help keep the game a quiet one. The stakes are provided by driving two clothespins or wooden pegs into blocks of ¾-in. wood, 10 or 12 in. square.

— TIRE SWING FOR TOTS —

Designed for very young children, the modern tire swing shown was made by cutting out a discarded automobile tire and turning it inside out so that the tread formed the seat. It boasts a seat back for safety, plus plenty of places for small hands to hang on tight. Cutting will be a great deal easier if you use a razor-sharp knife that has been heated. Ideally, you should alternate cutting with two knives so that one can be heating while the other is in use. A hot, sharp blade will cut through the heaviest tire, but be careful about overheating, for this can ruin the knife.

— TIRE SECTIONS PROTECT WORK —

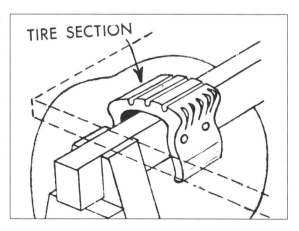

TIRE SECTION

To prevent the marring of woodwork that is being sanded or sawed on saw-horses, nail a few short tire sections to the top of each sawhorse stringer, as indicated in the illustration.

— OLD TIRE AS LADDER HELPER —

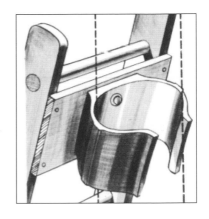

A section of an old tire casing can be attached to a ladder to serve as a collar. This permits you to rest the ladder against odd-shaped structures such as poles and trees, or any other narrow upright.

— RUBBER BANDS MADE FROM OLD INNER TUBES —

Old inner tubes from bicycles or other vehicles may be cut into rubber bands of various widths that will be found to give good service. The tubes should be laid flat on a hard piece of board or a piece of sheet zinc, and the bands cut off one at a time with a sharp knife held against the straightedge. In cutting them on wood, it is best to use a close-grained stock and to cut across the grain of the wood.

— A TIRE AS A HOSE HOLDER —

This hose holder, which can be easily rolled from place to place, is just an old tire casing. It's a real space saver for off-season storage, since a single tire can usually hold as much as 75 ft. of hose. If you're cramped for storage space, give this idea a try.

— TRUCK TIRE MAKES SAFE SANDBOX FOR SMALL TOTS —

Turned inside out and laid on the ground, an old truck tire provides a lasting sandbox, which will neither rot nor rust. And, the tire being slightly pliable, even the smallest child can fall against it without injury. Slits may be cut in the tire to take sticks to support a sunshade.

OLD TRUCK TIRE, INSIDE OUT

IF YOU WANT A SAFE, LASTING SANDBOX FOR CHILDREN, JUST GET AN OLD TRUCK TIRE AND TURN IT INSIDE OUT.

— TIRES PROTECT THE AXMAN —

Many individuals find splitting wood to be a down-to-earth method of invigorating exercise, but it requires some practice to handle the ax efficiently and safely. If you're a novice with an ax, one of the safest methods of splitting wood is to prop a log upright inside a couple of old tires. If you should miss the log, the tires will absorb the shock without moving. For a permanent workstation, affix a metal stake through the tires. This is an excellent use for old tires that are too worn out to use for anything else.

TREASURES *from* TRASH

— COUNTER BRUSH FOR A SHOP —

A very serviceable brush for use around a shop or other work area can be made from a discarded or worn-out push broom, as shown at *A*. Pull out and discard the bristles from one half of the brush, and shape the wood of that end with a knife or spokeshave to the form of a handle, and the brush will be formed as illustrated at *B*.

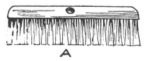

A DISCARDED PUSH BROOM SHAPED TO FORM A BRUSH
FOR A SHOP BENCH OR COUNTER.

— New Uses for Old Crayons —

Instead of pitching broken crayons into the nearest wastebasket, stop and examine their practical possibilities. There's a lot of life left in a piece of crayon even after being mangled, chewed, and stripped by your children. Start salvaging those pieces of colored wax now, and you'll be surprised by the countless ways they can aid you in the future. Here are a few to start, and you'll invent more as you go:

Novel decorations: Candles may be decorated easily in the home by melting the tips of colored crayons and allowing the soft wax to drip on them in various designs and formations. Simply heat the base of a candle to be decorated over the flame of another and press it into a dish or holder so that it is held firmly when the base hardens. The extra candle is then used to heat the crayons. For best results, only crayons of complementary or contrasting colors are used.

Restoring faded tapestries: Instead of discarding or storing away fine old tapestries that have faded, use crayons to recoup their original beauty. The first step is to wash the tapestry in mild, lukewarm suds and dry it on a flat surface. Press with a medium-hot iron to remove any wrinkles.

HERE IS AN EASY WAY TO DECORATE CANDLES WITH COLORFUL TRIMMINGS. MELT WAX CRAYONS OF COMPLEMENTARY OR CONTRASTING COLORS OVER A CANDLE SO THAT THE SOFT WAX WILL FLOW ALONG THE SIDES OF THE CANDLE TO FORM A RICH LAYER OF DRIPPINGS.

Coloring is done on a smooth, hard surface, using a well-pointed crayon. Hold the fabric taut between the thumb and fingers for even coloring, and avoid overlapping of different colors on adjacent areas. The colors may be more permanently set by covering the restored tapestry with wrapping paper and pressing it with a medium-hot iron.

IT'S NO TRICK AT ALL TO RESTORE FADED TAPESTRIES TO THEIR
ORIGINAL BEAUTY. THE FABRIC CAN BE RETINTED WITH COMMON
WAX CRAYONS. USE BRILLIANT COLORS FOR ARABIC, ITALIAN,
AND SIMILAR WEAVES. SLIGHTLY OFF-COLOR SHADES
USUALLY PASS UNNOTICED IN THE OVERALL PICTURE.

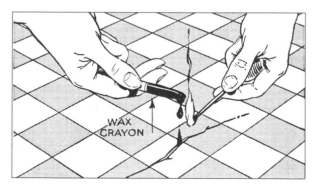

TO REPAIR CRACKS AND CHIPPED PLACES IN LINOLEUM,
MELT A WAX CRAYON OF THE SAME COLOR
INTO THE CRACK.

CRAYONS CAN BE USED TO WRITE ON
DOORS OF STOVES AND REFRIGERATORS
AS A REMINDER TO REMOVE
CERTAIN DISHES.

Time check: When baking or roasting, use a crayon to write on the oven door when the food was placed in the oven and when it should be taken out. Also, if sherbet or ice cream must be removed from the refrigerator at a definite time, write the hour on the refrigerator door. The marks are easily wiped off, and when you are in the kitchen they serve as a constant reminder.

Marking light bulbs: Burned-out light bulbs often become mixed with good ones, thus requiring that all bulbs be tested before returning those to be renewed. To save this trouble, marked burned-out bulbs with a crayon.

Marking darkroom trays: White enamel trays used in processing photo films may be marked with a black crayon to be easily identified in the dim light of a darkroom. On hard-rubber or plastic trays, which are usually of a dark color, yellow or red crayon will be more easily seen.

Needle holder: No time is wasted in looking for sewing needles if one is kept with each spool of thread. Just

Guide for cutting glass: To help keep a rule or straightedge from slipping while using it as a guide for a glass cutter, make heavy marks on the glass with a wax crayon. This will afford sufficient friction to hold the rule in place.

Patching linoleum: Very small cracks and chipped places in linoleum often can be repaired by melting a wax crayon into them. The crayon used should be of the same color as the linoleum around the crack or dent.

TO AVOID CONFUSING BURNED-OUT
LIGHT BULBS WITH GOOD ONES,
MARK THE BURNED-OUT ONES
WITH A CRAYON.

will find that a crayon mark on each side of the seam will do the trick. The solder will not flow beyond the marks unless an excessive amount is used, in which case it can be removed easily, as solder will not adhere to the metal under the marks. By taping two crayons together, a line can be made on each side of the seam in one operation.

To decorate flowerpots: Flowerpots can be decorated with bands or designs marked on them lightly with chalk or soft pencil, after which crayons are used to fill in the colors between the lines. The texture of a clay pot will give the design a soft, pebbly finish that will blend readily with its surroundings.

General crayon suggestions: Wrapping crayons with tape reinforces them to withstand greater pressure and protects them from breaking and chipping or soiling your hands. The tape is wrapped spirally around the crayon and peeled off as necessary, to expose more of the tip.

To keep wax crayons pointed, dip the ends in hot water to soften the wax, and then rotate them between the tips of the thumb and first finger to draw them to points. Or twist a strip of tin and tack it to the wall; the free end provides a blade. To point a crayon, insert it in the blade and turn.

press a short piece of crayon into the hole in the center of the spool, and stick the needle in the crayon.

Polish for shoe soles: Often, after cleaning a pair of white shoes, the soles become smeared with polish. Ordinary brown polish does not always cover the white satisfactorily, and a damp rag sometimes smears it worse. A wax crayon rubbed over the spots will completely wipe away all traces in a matter of seconds.

In the workshop: Beginners who experience difficulty in confining solder to a narrow, neat band when making long seams in sheet metal

— SALVAGING DRAIN OIL FROM CANS OPENED AT FILLING STATION —

An old brake drum placed over a pail is used by the owner of a filing station to save the oil that adheres to the sides of sealed cans when they are emptied. Letting the cans remain inverted in the drum for several hours assures that every bit of the oil will drain out.

— PLASTIC SQUEEZE DISPENSERS PUMP AIR, LIQUID SOAP, AND WATER —

Plastic dispenser bottles can be adapted to many uses around the home after serving their original purpose. A ketchup dispenser bottle, shown in the photos, can be used as a miniature bellows for cleaning away dust from inside a camera or as a hand dispenser for liquid hand soap. The latter is clamped to the wall with a sheet-metal strip. Also shown is an empty squeeze bottle designed for talcum that, when filled with water, will throw a stream 5 ft. away. This makes it great for wetting down anything, fine for watering plants, and practical as a "poor-man's" windshield squirter, which can be kept in the glove compartment. Because the cap is sealed on, the bottle is easily filled by squeezing it and then siphoning the water through the holes in the cap.

— BARREL-STAVE HAMMOCK —

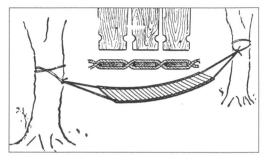

CHEAP AND COMFORTABLE HAMMOCK.

A hammock made of barrel staves is more comfortable than one would think, considering the nature of the material employed in making it. Good, smooth staves should be selected for this purpose. If one cares to go to a little trouble, a thorough sandpapering will make a great improvement. Cut half circles out of each stave and pass ropes around the ends. When finished, the weight will then be supported by four ropes at each end, which allows the use of small-sized ropes, such as clotheslines. A hammock of this kind may be left out in the rain without injury.

— REUSING NYLON STOCKINGS —

Nylon stockings are excellent holders for mothballs and other moth repellants. Drop a half dozen or so mothballs into a stocking, and hang the stocking on a hook in the closet where the family's off-season clothes are stored and your clothes will be fine in the spring.

— EMPTY CAULKING CARTRIDGE MAKES PUMP —

When it's empty, you might not think a caulking cartridge could be of much use, but that's where you're wrong. Fitted with a piston and handle, it becomes a dandy little pump.

With it you can fill a gear case with grease, suck the gas out of a power mower when putting it away for the season, or bail those last few cupfuls of water from your boat. You'll also find it handy when you

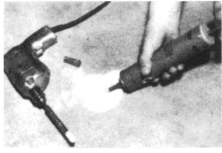

DRAWING UP ON THE
PUMP HANDLE WILL
SUCK LEFTOVER GAS
FROM A POWER MOWER
WHEN STORING IT FOR
WINTER.

PUSHING IN ON THE HANDLE WILL CAUSE
THE PUMP TO BLOW A STRONG JET OF
AIR, FINE FOR BLOWING DUST FROM A
DRILLED HOLE.

THE PUMP BECOMES A
GREASE GUN BY FILLING
THE CARTRIDGE WITH
LUBRICANT AND SQUIRTING
THE GREASE OUT OF THE
TAPERED NOZZLE.

need to blow chips or dust from a hole drilled in concrete.

It's simple enough to make the pump as shown in the drawing. The piston consists of a threaded rod fitted with two plastic cups, placed back to back, with a plywood washer between. One of these cups is in each cartridge—it's what forces the caulk out of the nozzle.

The pump works best when the cups rub firmly against the sides of the tube. By tightening the nuts a little, you can ensure a better fit. A drop of oil or a little grease on the cups will improve the seal and ease pumping.

When the pump is to be used only as a blowgun, one plastic cup on the piston (with its lip toward the nozzle) is enough. For extra reach, a length of plastic hose can be forced over the nozzle. To start a siphon, you hold the pump at a point lower than the level of the liquid and slowly pull up on the piston. This fills the hose with liquid, and if you then remove the hose from the pump, the liquid should siphon by itself.

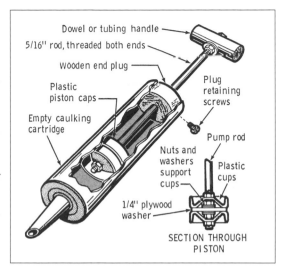

Dowel or tubing handle
5/16" rod, threaded both ends
Wooden end plug
Plastic piston caps
Empty caulking cartridge
Plug retaining screws
Pump rod
Nuts and washers support cups
Plastic cups
1/4" plywood washer
SECTION THROUGH PISTON

— COPPER FLOAT PROVIDES CANDY DISH —

Something novel in the way of covered candy dishes can be had by assembling a flush-tank float, a lamp-base cap, and a knob-type drawer pull. The seam around the center of the copper float is first broken with a file to separate the float into two parts. This leaves a small lip around the rim of each half. A ¼-in. copper strip is soldered around the inside of the rim of the bottom half, which will serve as the bowl. The strip should project slightly above the rim, to aid in locating the upper half of the float, or cover. The lamp-base cap is fastened to the threaded stud at the bottom of the bowl with a screw and washer. Then, a hole is drilled through the top of the cover to permit attaching the drawer pull. If all parts are of copper, simply polish the candy dish, but if different metals are used, it is best to have the unit plated.

— NEW USES FOR EMPTY SPOOLS —

HALVES OF SPOOL AID IN HOLDING SMALL ROD OR TUBING IN VISE

SMALL SPOOLS DIPPED IN GLUE AND COATED WITH ABRASIVE CAN BE USED FOR SANDING DELICATE SCROLL WORK

REWINDING SPOOL WHICH IS FORCED ON SHORT ROD AND HELD IN DRILL CHUCK

SPOOL IS FORCED ON SHORT ROD

USED AS A BEARING FOR LIGHT SHAFTS

SPOOLS FITTED IN THE ENDS OF A LENGTH OF PIPE AND DRILLED FOR SHAFT, MAKING A SERVICEABLE ROLLER FOR SMALL DOLLY

KEYED ON MOTOR SHAFT, A SPOOL WILL SERVE AS A DRIVE PULLEY FOR FLAT OR ROUND BELT

SPOOL SPLIT LENGTHWISE AND THE HALVES TAPED OVER BUCKET BAIL WILL SAVE THE HANDS

WOOD SCREW-HOLE BUTTON

WOOD PLUG

THREE-CORNERED FILE DRIVEN INTO SLOTTED SPOOL MAKES GOOD SAW JOINTER

LARGE SPOOL WITH CENTER DRILLED OUT AND PLUGGED AT ONE END MAKES HANDY HOLDER FOR SMALL DRILLS

SPOOLS CUT IN HALF AND COUNTERBORED FOR SCREW, MAKE ATTRACTIVE ANTIQUE DRAWER PULLS, OR HANDLES FOR SCREEN DOORS

— Mailing Tube Holds Small Parts, for Easy Dispensing —

Plugged at both ends with wooden disks and having an access opening cut into the side, a mailing tube makes an ideal dispenser for nails, tacks, screws, and other small parts found around the workshop. The detail shows how a baffle plate is fastened inside the tube to control the flow of parts. The reservoir space above the baffle permits the storage of large quantities of items.

— Coconut-shell Trays —

Trays for holding matches or other articles may be made of coconut shells by cutting them to appropriate sizes and smoothing the surface to a polish. The tray shown in the sketch was made in this manner, as were a number of match trays, which were fitted with small sheet-metal dishes. The outside of the shell is first scraped as smooth as possible and

sandpapered, and then oil-polished, producing a beautiful finish.

— MILK CARTONS SERVE AS PAINT CUPS —

Try cutting down a cardboard milk container to the desired size instead of using tin cups or cans in which to mix a little paint for small jobs. The cartons are leakproof, and can be discarded after the job has been completed. Be careful to disregard them safely, as many paints are flammable.

— RECYCLING OLD FILM CANISTERS —

Campers will find 35-mm film canisters handy for carrying many things. Being watertight, they're fine for matches. You can also glue foil over the opening and punch holes to make salt and pepper shakers. Sealed, they will also float if accidently dropped from a canoe. Many a camper has spent a cold, wet night without dry matches.

Striker strip

INDEX